Assessing Academic
Library Performance

Medical Library Association Books

The Medical Library Association (MLA) publishes state-of-the-art books that enhance health care, support professional development, improve library services, and promote research throughout the world.

MLA books are dynamic resources for librarians in hospitals, medical research practice, corporate libraries, and other settings. These invaluable publications provide medical librarians, health care professionals, and patients with accurate information that can improve outcomes and save lives.

Medical Library Association Books Panel

The MLA Books Panel is responsible for (1) monitoring publishing trends within the industry; (2) exploring new concepts in publications by actively soliciting and proposing ideas for new publications; and (3) coordinating publishing efforts to achieve the best utilization of MLA resources. Each MLA book is directly administered from its inception by the MLA Books Panel, composed of MLA members with expertise spanning the breadth of health sciences librarianship.

About the Medical Library Association

The Medical Library Association (MLA) is a global, nonprofit educational organization, with a membership of more than 400 institutions and 3,000 professionals in the health information field. Since 1898, MLA has fostered excellence in the professional practice and leadership of health sciences library and information professionals to enhance health care, education, and research throughout the world. MLA educates health information professionals, supports health information research, promotes access to the world's health sciences information, and works to ensure that the best health information is available to all.

Recently Published MLA Books Include

3D Printing in Medical Libraries: A Crash Course in Supporting Innovation in Healthcare by Jennifer Herron

Diversity and Inclusion in Libraries: A Call to Action and Strategies for Success Edited by Shannon D. Jones and Beverly Murphy

Framing Health Care Instruction: An Information Literacy Handbook for the Health Sciences by Lauren M. Young and Elizabeth G. Hinton

The Clinical Medical Librarian's Handbook Edited by Judy C. Stribling

The Engaged Health Sciences Library Liaison Edited by Lindsay Alcock and Kelly Thormodson

A History of Medical Libraries and Medical Librarianship: From John Shaw Billings to the Digital Era by Michael R. Kronenfeld and Jennie Jacobs Kronenfeld

Planning and Promoting Events in Health Sciences Libraries: Success Stories and Best Practices Edited by Shalu Gillum and Natasha Williams

Great Library Events: From Planning to Promotion to Evaluation by Mary Grace Flaherty

Assessing Academic Library Performance

A Handbook

Edited by
Holt Zaugg

ROWMAN & LITTLEFIELD
Lanham • Boulder • New York • London

Published by Rowman & Littlefield
A wholly owned subsidary of The Rowman & Littlefield Publishing Group, Inc.
4501 Forbes Boulevard, Suite 200, Lanham, Maryland 20706
www.rowman.com

6 Tinworth Street, London SE11 5AL, United Kingdom

British Library Cataloguing in Publication Information Available

Library of Congress Cataloging-in-Publication Data
Names: Zaugg, Holt, 1959- editor.
Title: Assessing academic library performance : a handbook / Holt Zaugg.
Description: Lanham : Rowman & Littlefield, [2021] | Series: Medical
  Library Association books | Includes bibliographical references and
  index. | Summary: "This authoritative guide to conducting assessments
  within academic libraries is organized into four section: services,
  resources, spaces, and personnel. The book serves as a springboard to
  adopt, adapt, or create assessments to describe a library's value and to
  plan for improvement"— Provided by publisher.
Identifiers: LCCN 2021019528 (print) | LCCN 2021019529 (ebook) | ISBN
  9781538149232 (paperback) | ISBN 9781538149249 (epub)
Subjects: LCSH: Academic libraries—Evaluation. | Academic
  libraries—United States—Evaluation. | Academic
  libraries—Evaluation—Case studies. | Academic libraries—United
  States—Evaluation—Case studies.
Classification: LCC Z675.U5 A5975 2021 (print) | LCC Z675.U5 (ebook) |
  DDC 027.7—dc23
LC record available at https://lccn.loc.gov/2021019528
LC ebook record available at https://lccn.loc.gov/2021019529

This book is dedicated to my wife, my family, my parents, and my in-laws— all of who helped me become who I am today and, more importantly, who tolerated my drive to learn through assessment and evaluation

~

Contents

~

List of Figures, Tables, and Chapter Appendices

Figures

Tables

Chapter Appendices

Preface

This book is for those who have specific responsibilities to conduct assessments within academic libraries or who conduct assessments as part of their job. It is organized into four sections: services (chapters 2–5), resources (chapters 6–8), spaces (chapters 9–12), and personnel relationships (chapters 13–16), bookended by chapters that provide an assessment framework and look forward to how library assessments may describe value and assist planning.

Each section begins with an introductory chapter outlining assessments and considerations for each type of assessment based on four components: design, data collection, data analysis, and dissemination. While specific to academic libraries, the principles could be applied to other libraries and to other nonlibrary institutions. It is also important to note that book sections and assessment components are not mutually exclusive. What happens in one section or assessment component often influences and interacts with other sections or assessment components. Each section is briefly described:

Services refers to all of the inward and outward interactions that help patrons learn about and use everything the library offers physically or virtually and helps library employees do their jobs more effectively. John Spencer discusses the steps taken to assess a new information desk and its services.

Susan Montgomery gathered quantitative and qualitative feedback from students to help assess and improve their library's website. Fields et al. discuss the evaluation of a repository shared by several Maryland institutions to determine its value and to improve service.

Resource assessments focus on access to and development of the physical and virtual resources collected by libraries. Gregory Nelson describes the prototyping processes used to "weed" the science and engineering collection to a third of its original size. Berenika and Keith Webster use their experiences in publishing and libraries to help build a negotiation playbook.

Space assessments examine physical and virtual library spaces, especially in terms of improving user access and considerations on how changes affect other library aspects. Barbara Ghilardi describes the development of an assessment toolkit for libraries of all sizes to evaluate spaces. Joelle Pitts discusses a space assessment "pre-op," structural-level assessment of library spaces and facilities that provides a foundation from which any space project can begin. Laura Spears and her colleagues at the University of Florida examine how the initial results from a spatial analysis and intercept survey assessment inform library renovations.

Personnel relationships examine the interactions among library employees and between library employees and patrons that facilitate communications. Tijerno et al. describe a professional development journey of two library employees. Mentors helped them improve their skill levels and abilities to assist other librarians in their duties. Martin and Thompson describe an effort to map all library services. The result improved library employee understandings of the work done by others and strengthened communication lines by defining common terms. Zaugg describes a communication network analysis that indicates the level and intensity of communications among library employees.

Each section stands alone as it provides ideas on types of assessments and how to conduct them. The book serves as a springboard to adopt, adapt, or create assessments to describe a library's value and to plan for improvement.

~

CHAPTER ONE

Assessment Framework

Holt Zaugg

Assessment does not magically happen. It requires planning and execution. An assessment framework helps explain its purpose, focus, and tools to be used. A library assessment framework for examining library spaces, services, resources, and personnel relationships helps library employees collect data from patrons to assess the library's value to the university community and identify trends and patterns in usage (Allen et al., 2018; Dunya and De Groote, 2019).

An effective assessment framework assists both short- and long-term decision-making, while describing the library's value to the university community. In times of budget cuts and limited resources, the ability to indicate a library's value is essential. While describing the library's value may not spare budget cuts, it may result in cuts that are not as deep.

This chapter discusses the purpose of an assessment framework and provides several examples. This framework is referenced throughout the book as a means to design and conduct assessments. The chapter ends with discussion of components and several assessment tools that facilitate the development and use of an assessment framework used in assessments.

Assessment Framework

An assessment framework serves several purposes. It includes an iterative nature that helps short- and long-term decision-making. It guides employees, who do not have an assessment background, but want to improve what they do through assessment. It provides different perspectives of everything that is assessed in the library. Finally, it describes library value by linking library activities to university aims and goals.

Strategic planning is a series of short- and long-term decision-making. Short-term decisions are the small, incremental steps that complete long-term plans. Long-term decisions are informed by identifying trends and patterns that provide a broad view of the library. Library leadership and employees use both to set complementary goals for improvement.

All assessments are iterative, only the time period for reassessment changes (Zaugg, 2018). Repeated assessments allow decision-makers to adjust practices, policies, and spaces to students' and faculty members' changing needs. The frequency of assessment depends on what is being evaluated. For example, deciding what type of furniture should go in a group study room will happen rarely, perhaps once in a decade. Gate counts are assessed daily. Everything else is between these two timeframes. The next assessment iteration depends on how frequently something changes, and the scope of the trend or pattern being examined.

An assessment framework guides library employees who seek to evaluate their work assignment and clarifies the assessment components that fit into each assessment. When all employees work toward the common goal of improvement, a community of assessment is created (Streatfield et al., 2019). This community provides a transparent forum representing the voices of library employees and patrons, especially the perspective of those who, at times, feel marginalized (Clarke and Schoonmaker, 2019; Corrall, 2017; Miller, 2018). Marginalization excluded people because of special learning needs, disabilities, or recent life changes (e.g., being recently married or divorced with children). Marginalization differentiates library employees by gender, race, position, or rank. A community of assessment counters marginalization by drawing an inclusive circle that is flexible, adaptable, and focused on all library stakeholders. Assessments do not reflect a winner or a loser, or a right or a wrong attitude but merely describe what is happening in the library with a view toward improvement. This assessment attitude bends library elements and personal attitudes toward an inclusive environment that benefits all (Kaufman et al., 2018; Schwieder and Hinchcliffe, 2018).

Finally, the assessment framework provides a clear connection between library processes and university goals. In doing so, it justifies budget expenditures and needs. If the library is the heart of the college community, library assessments are the measures that determine just how healthy the heart is.

Assessment Framework Examples

With multiple assessment frameworks available from a variety of disciplines, each library modifies and implements a framework that works best for their circumstances. Assessment frameworks may be known by different names, but each provides a foundation for developing and conducting an assessment. The assessment framework provides the broad foundation for conducting all assessments. An assessment plan contains the specific assessment details of what, how, when, and by whom. Several assessment frameworks are provided to illustrate different types of assessment frameworks.

Hogan and Hutson (2018) at the Longsdale Library use a five-year rotating assessment plan that supports sustainable assessment. The five steps of the assessment are (1) gathering data, (2) analyzing and interpreting the data, (3) planning for improvement, (4) sharing the data and the plan, and (5) implementing the plan. The fifth step returns librarians back to the starting point of collecting data, and the cycle repeats itself. The strength of this plan is its iterative nature and the meshing of assessment, planning, and accountability.

At the University of Tennessee, Kaufman et al. (2018) propose a framework centered on six best practices for conducting a library assessment. The best practices include:

1. Undergo the university institutional review board (IRB) process that allows evaluators to disseminate findings beyond the university library and ensures participants' rights and privacy are protected.
2. Conduct a pilot of the assessment, especially with larger or complex assessments, so that any glitches may be worked out prior to the main data collection.
3. Choose effective assessment tools that will also be the least intrusive.
4. Remember that all feedback is informative feedback. Negative feedback indicates what library employees should do less. Positive feedback indicates what should be done more.
5. Choose an assessment framework or model that fits the library's climate, that fosters collaboration and collegiality, and that library employees will support.

6. Learn from others by collaborating with library employees and campus faculty so that costly mistakes are avoided. Collaboration also helps see things from different perspectives.
7. These practices fit together in an iterative process to ensure that assessments are planned and conducted well.

At New Zealand's University of Otago, Hart and Amos (2018) proposed a matrix assessment rubric model with four stages of assessment in conjunction with five levels of capability. The five assessment stages include: (1) stating the assessment objectives, (2) describing the methods for collecting data, (3) describing data analysis and interpretation, and (4) stating how the results are used. They apply each stage at differing capability levels, ranging from one-off assessments with ill-defined processes that are somewhat chaotic and dependent on an individual for continuous improvement, to ongoing assessments that continue regardless of personnel. Innovative assessment processes are enabled by feedback and technology. A level of assessment maturity is indicated by where assessments align on this rubric with the intent of moving assessments from a novice to an expert level.

The Harold B. Lee Library at Brigham Young University employs an assessment framework with three dimensions: the assessment tasks, the types of assessments, and assessment tools. Each assessment discusses tasks (design, data collection, data analysis, dissemination), links to library and university aims and goals, and reference to assessment tools that may be used. This framework provides an underlying structure for all assessments that create consistent assessments across all library departments and levels of employee assessment expertise.

Each library should choose and adapt an assessment framework to meet the needs and culture of their specific library. While the assessment tools are quite universal across disciplines and assessment formats, the types of assessment are specific to each academic library and focus on the library's unique characteristics. While each framework mentioned above has merit and fits the respective library, the Lee Library Assessment Framework is used as the model to frame discussions of library assessments in this text. Book sections correspond to one of the types of assessment (service, resources, spaces, or personnel relationships), with an introductory chapter discussing the assessment tasks unique to each type of assessment, followed by specific assessment examples. For this reason, the Lee Library Assessment Framework is discussed in greater detail than the other example frameworks.

Lee Library Assessment Framework

The Harold B. Lee Library's assessment framework has three dimensions and encompasses all library assessments, connecting each assessment to library and university aims and goals.

Assessment Tasks

There are four tasks necessary for all assessments: design, data collection, data analysis, and dissemination (see figure 1.1).

Design

The first assessment task connects the assessment to library and university goals as evaluators plan all aspects of the assessment. It includes the scope of the assessment and the questions that the assessment seeks to answer, and it helps with the development of the other three assessment tasks.

An essential focus of the design task is the *triangle of assessment*: speed, cost, and depth. *Speed* refers to how quickly the assessment can be completed, typically within a semester or a school year at an academic library. *Cost* refers to both time and monetary expenses incurred during the assessment,

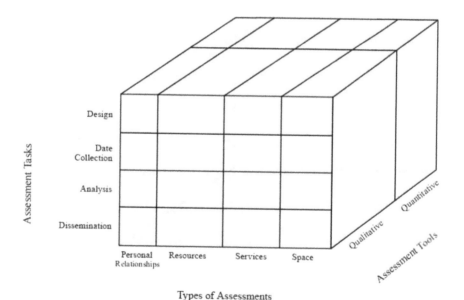

Figure 1.1. Model of the Assessment Framework. Zaugg, 2020. With permission of Taylor & Francis.

including assessment personnel, wages, equipment, and incentives. *Depth* refers to insights gained from greater detail and disaggregation of data. Depth connects patrons to what they need and employees to what they need to do.

In any assessment, evaluators can only successfully do two of the three points in the triangle of assessment. Designing an assessment determines which of these two points will be used and which one needs additional attention. For example, an assessment can be executed quickly and at a low cost, but it will not have much depth.

Data Collection

The second assessment task is the actual collection of data using the tool chosen in design, be it a survey, observations, or some other assessment tool.

Data Analysis

For the third assessment task to be effective, the appropriate analysis methods must be identified prior to collecting data, otherwise the collected data may be difficult, if not impossible, to analyze. Analyses range from simple descriptive data to statistically significant findings or rich data descriptions. The analysis may pertain to a single assessment or demonstrate pattern and trend changes necessary for decision-making.

Data Dissemination

The fourth assessment task requires that all results, good or bad, need to be shared with all pertinent stakeholders, including those from other universities via conferences or journal articles. Reports should be consistent, easy-to-read, and stored in an easily accessible repository. This openness promotes a culture of assessment and allows library employees to learn from previous assessments. Evaluators have a responsibility to share knowledge gained from assessments with others who may benefit from this knowledge.

Types of Assessments

The library's aims, goals, and needs determine the types of assessment that are needed to meet the unique future needs of each library. For example, if a library is about to undergo extensive renovations, more space assessments may be needed than if a library just completed renovations. Assessments range from a single unit to the entire library. The type of assessment should fit, but not extend beyond, the scope of the assessment. As an example, personnel relationships may explore communication networks and patterns throughout the library, but it should not stretch beyond communication patterns to assess individual employees for year-end reports or advancement decisions. Most library assessments include individual or the combined library aspects of services, resources, spaces, and personnel relationships.

Assessment Tools

The type of assessment tool used in an assessment is determined by the questions that need to be answered, who the participants are, and how intrusive the tool is. Most assessments blend qualitative and quantitative tools to provide a more complete picture of what is being assessed, a process known as *triangulation* (Glowacka, 2019; Sanchez-Rodriguez, 2017; Schwieder and Hinchliffe, 2018).

Think of five blind men who each examine a different part of an elephant. One touches the elephant's ear, another its trunk, a third its tusk, a fourth its leg, and the fifth its tail. If each blind man were to describe what an elephant is most like based only on his personal experience, each would be correct, in part. Combined, each perspective offers a more complete description of the elephant. However, even with this combined data from each perspective, much is still unknown about the elephant! So it is with assessments. While each perspective or assessment tool provides information on the aspect of the library being examined, each assessment is an incomplete picture, but it is better than no picture at all!

Additional Assessment Components

Several components that provide a broad view of assessments are helpful in designing an assessment framework and conducting assessments. Think of seeing your home from thirty thousand feet in the air and then zooming in to see your front yard. These components help those conducting and using an assessment to zoom into and out of their unique situation. These components include library personas, a library impact map, and a data inventory.

Library Personas

Adopted from the world of advertising and marketing, personas provide descriptions of a group of individuals as if the group were a single person. The descriptions may be quite detailed, including a faux picture along with a biographic description, or they may be simple, with a name that reflects the common behavior. A persona description simply focuses on the common behaviors of a group of people so that an evaluator may think of a single individual's needs instead of accounting for all the people in the group (Nagy, 2013; Pruitt and Grudin, 2003).

Zaugg and Rackham (2016) identified and validated ten personas, evaluated how they used the library, and estimated what percentage of students made up each persona. A later validation effort determined that these personas were found at another academic library (Zaugg and Ziegenfuss, 2018), indicating the potential for universality among academic libraries. Personas are not stable within any individual but change depending on the student's needs. For example, a student may seek a place in the library where she or he can quietly work uninterrupted on learning tasks, the Focuser persona, but change to relaxing and visiting with friends, the Socializer persona, after finishing the tasks. Each persona has specific needs of the library, which enables evaluators to seek input and feedback from a particular persona group.

Library Impact Map

Initially proposed by Megan Oakleaf (2012), the library impact map (LIM) has a twofold purpose. First, it connects library units with university goals and areas of focus by indicating the degree to which data is collected (ranging from not collected to collected, used, and shared with stakeholders). Second, the LIM indicates which units may start collecting or using data to inform decisions (Zaugg, 2015). If the unit is already collecting, using, and sharing data, the evaluator may work with the unit to describe the library's value and help with decision-making and planning. Periodically repeated LIMs provide an indication of the degree to which the library is (or is not) developing a culture of assessment.

Data Inventory

A data inventory provides a way to easily locate and access the types of library collected data, identify who collects the data, determine how often the data is collected, and indicate where the data is stored (Zaugg et al., 2017). If desired, part of the data inventory may ask library employees what types of library data they currently do not collect, but would like to, that would be helpful in the discharge of their duties. Knowing these things helps expedite data collection.

Assessment Tools

This section only provides a sample of commonly used assessment tools—a bit like a taster at a grocery store—just enough information to encourage you to try them out. Each tool is briefly described along with its strengths and weaknesses.

Interviews

There are multiple types of interviews, ranging from an intercept interview in which a passersby is asked to participate in a brief interview, to one-on-one interviews, which typically occur in a private setting (Bernard, 2006). Interviews are typically audio-recorded for accuracy and to prevent bias that may result if the interviewee is influenced by the interviewer taking notes. Interviews focus on participants' experience or behavior, feelings, values, knowledge, or expertise (Beebe, 2001; Bernard, 2006; Creswell, 2007; Matthews, 2007).

Advantages

An interviewer can give personalized attention to the interviewee, who may speak more freely in a one-on-one interview, particularly if discussing a sensitive subject. Using open-ended and follow-up questions, the interviewer can explore issues that come up in the interview more deeply, thus providing greater depth to the evaluator's understanding. Interviews are often used with other assessment tools to improve understanding.

Disadvantages

Scheduling, conducting, and transcribing an interview has costs in terms of time, money, and mental ability. The cost of interviewing increases with the number and length of interviews. Transcribing an interview recording can extend the interview time by three to four times. An interviewer must also exert mental effort to keep each interview session fresh and novel. Imaging asking the same questions of twenty people over a few days—are we there yet?

Focus Groups

Focus groups are often thought of as group interviews. They concentrate on a specific topic or a few related topics with participants who are chosen using demographic indicators (e.g., age, gender, university status, major). Groups may be homogeneous (e.g., just freshmen) or more heterogeneous (e.g., all undergraduate students). Typically, two people conduct a focus group: a moderator, who is front and center in the focus group, asks the questions and engages the participants, and a facilitator or technician, who remains in the background, records the conversations, and takes notes so participants will not be distracted or influenced by note-taking and recording. Video recordings are often used for accuracy and to clearly identify who is talking and the nonverbal communication of all participants (Beebe, 2001; Bernard, 2006; Matthews, 2007).

Advantages

Focus groups interview a greater number of people in less time than it takes to interview all participants individually. Focus groups also allow evaluators to access the collective knowledge and understanding of a specific group. Comments from one participant will often stir the memory of another participant, resulting in a robust, synergistic conversation (Beebe, 2001; Creswell, 2007).

Disadvantages

Transcribing a focus group takes more time than a one-on-one interview because multiple speakers, each with nonverbal communication, inform the discussion. The moderator also needs specific skills to conduct a focus group effectively. In addition to asking the questions, the moderator may need to encourage some participants to comment or stop others from dominating the conversation. If there are strong differing opinions, the moderator must remain completely neutral while ensuring that all opinions are respected. Finally, focus groups do not allow for anonymity, as participants can hear each other's comments. Participants should be cautioned not to repeat other participants' comments outside of the group.

Surveys

Surveys allow for easy and rapid data collection, which target a specific group, a broad sample of a population, or a convenience sample. Surveys may be administered in person or online. Online survey software often allows evaluators to filter what questions are and are not seen depending on immediate participant responses. Most library surveys are created by employees to quickly gather information about some aspect of the library.

A variety of questions may be asked in a survey, including simple alternate-response questions (yes–no, do–don't), rating questions ("To what degree do you feel . . . ?"), and open-ended questions. A survey's size may range from a single question to over a hundred questions (Beebe, 2001; Bernard, 2006; Matthews, 2007).

Advantages

Surveys enable evaluators to ask questions in a very short time period and allow, with incentives, a reasonable response that is indicative of the general population of students regarding a wide variety of topics. Similar surveys that are repeated over time facilitate statistical analysis of change.

Disadvantages

Writing survey questions requires skill and practice using a common understandable language that is free of jargon and conflicting or leading comments. To ensure that a survey is understandable and unbiased, questions should be piloted or reviewed by others.

Because people are inundated with all types of surveys, they may not be willing to participate unless there is a significant incentive. The length of a survey affects response rate: As the number of survey questions increases, the response rate diminishes. Some students may love taking surveys, which creates an inherent bias. Not all survey collection methods are equal or affordable. Students' contact information (e.g., their email adresses) may be difficult, if not impossible, to get. There may be institutional policies that require extra approval levels to conduct surveys.

The largest disadvantage of surveys is that people may not always tell the truth—intentionally or unintentionally—as they may want to provide the responses that they think evaluators are looking for or that they think are the most correct. Or they may not always accurately recall what they did or how they did it. The result is the same whether responses are inaccurate or incomplete.

Ethnographies

Borrowed and adapted from anthropology (Bernard, 2006; Creswell, 2007; Matthews, 2007), ethnographies, combined with other assessment tools, allow evaluators to see how students interact in the library. In an ethnography, an evaluator typically follows or observes the student during a structured or unstructured visit to the library. An unstructured ethnography watches a student as they go about their business, whereas a structured ethnography provides the students specific tasks. The evaluator may record the participant, take field notes, and ask questions when necessary. If a specific area of the library is being assessed, evaluators may set up a camera and record what is happening and how student interactions unfold.

Advantages

Ethnographies provide one of the clearest views of student actions and interactions in the library's environment. With recorded ethnographies, participants cannot leave out elements of their experience, either intentionally or unintentionally, and the evaluator may watch the video several times to gain a deeper understanding of several aspects of the student's visit to the library. If a follow-up interview is used with the ethnography, the evaluator can show some or all of the video and ask the student questions.

Disadvantages

One of the greatest disadvantages of ethnographies is the time and cost needed to conduct an ethnography and analyze the data. Additionally, the student may alter his or her actions because of the recorded observations. If an ethnography is video recorded, additional levels of notification (typically a poster or consent) are needed.

Observations

While observation is a significant part of an ethnography, it may also be used independently to examine a broad group or single out a specific student. One method of observation uses a secret shopper, an accomplice who approaches a specific service with a predetermined request to determine how well the service is functioning or to influence desired interactions (Beebe, 2001; Bernard, 2006; Matthews, 2007). Surveys or interviews can be added to observation to provide insight into particular actions.

Advantages

Many of the advantages listed with ethnographies also apply to observations as they provide insights into students' library usage and interactions.

Disadvantages

Observation takes time and money to conduct and analyze. In direct observations, evaluators may become distracted or unfocused and miss something that happened. Observers must be able to blend in and be as unobtrusive as possible so they do not influence students' behavior. While the secret-shopper observation is effective, it requires a host of provisions because it uses deception that prevents student consent and may violate students' privacy rights.

Summary

An assessment framework provides an understanding that helps all library employees conduct assessments that create a triangulated picture of some aspect of an academic library. The three dimensions of the Harold B. Lee Library Assessment Framework—the assessment tasks, the types of assessments, and assessment tools—provide a context to plan and conduct multiple assessments. While no assessment is perfect, library assessments provide insights into what has happened in the past, what is happening now, and suggest future changes to improve library-patron interactions.

The overall goal of using an assessment framework is to advance the work of assessing and improving interactions within a library (Allen et al., 2018). Developing an attitude of continuous improvement within the library requires all library employees to grow a culture of assessment and learn from each other. All library employees should actively contribute to assessments in the library and build the assessment knowledge base. When library employees need to make a decision, the first question becomes, "What data is there to support that decision?" Assessment data indicates the library's value and refutes those who would question the need or value of libraries within the university community.

References

Allen, E. J., Weber, R. K., and Howerton, W. (2018). Library assessment research: A content comparison from three American library journals. *Publications*, 6(1), 1–22. https://doi.org/10.3390/PUBLICATIONS6010012.

Beebe, J. (2001). *Rapid assessment process: An introduction*. AltaMira Press; Rowman and Littlefield Publishers, Inc.

Bernard, H. R. (2006). *Research methods in anthropology: Qualitative and quantitative approaches* (fourth edition). AltaMira Press; Rowman and Littlefield Publishers, Inc.

Clarke, R. I., and Schoonmaker, S. (2019). Metadata for diversity: Identification and implications of potential access points for diverse library resources. *Journal of Documentation*, 76(1), 173–96. https://doi.org/10.1108/JD-01-2019-0003.

Corrall, S. (2017). Library space assessment methods: Perspectives of new information professionals. *Information and Learning Science*, 119(1–2), 39–63. https://doi.org/10.1108/ILS-10-2017-0097.

Creswell, J. W. (2007). *Qualitative inquiry and research design: Choosing among five approaches*. Sage Publications.

Dunya, B., and De Groote, S. (2019). Revision of an academic library user experience survey. *Performance Measurement and Metrics*, 20(1), 48–59. https://doi.org/10.1108/PMM-10-2018-0026.

Glowacka, E. (2019). Research on the impact of academic libraries—Areas, methods, indicators. *Library Management*, 40(8–9), 583–92. https://doi.org/10.1108/LM-02-2019-0005.

Hart, S., and Amos, H. (2018). The Library Assessment Capability Maturity Model: A means of optimizing how libraries measure effectiveness. *Evidence Based Library and Information Practice*, 13(4), 31–49. https://doi.org/10.18438/eblip29471.

Hogan, S., and Hutson, J. (2018). Assessing access services: Building a five-year plan for sustainable assessment. *Journal of Access Services*, 15(2–3), 80–88. https://doi.org/10.1080/15367967.2018.1479189.

Kaufman, J., Dosch, B., and Clement, K. A. (2018). No failure, just feedback: A reflection on experiential space assessment in an academic library. *Serials Review*, 44(3), 221–27. https://doi.org/10.1080/00987913.2018.1513749.

Matthews, J. R. (2007). *The evaluation and measurement of library services*. Libraries Unlimited; Greenwood Publishing Group.

Miller, L. N. (2018). What is helpful (and not) in the strategic planning process? An exploratory survey and literature review. *Library Leadership and Management*, 32(3), 1–27.

Nagy, B. (2013, December 3). *How to breathe life into personas*. Boxes and arrows. https://boxesandarrows.com/how-to-breathe-life-into-personas.

Oakleaf, M. (2012). *Academic library value: The impact starter kit*. American Library Association.

Pruitt, J., and Grudin, J. (2003, June). Personas: Practice and theory. DUX '03: Proceedings of the 2003 Conference on Designing for User Experience, San Francisco, CA, 1–15.

Sanchez-Rodriguez, N. A. (2017). Mixed methods of assessment: Measures of enhancing library services in academia. *Collection and Curation*, 37(3), 111–18. http://doi.org/10.1108/CC-09-2017-0042.

Schwieder, D., and Hinchliffe, L. J. (2018). A multilevel approach for library value assessment. *College and Research Libraries*, 79(3), 424–36. https://doi.org/10.5860/crl.79.3.424.

Streatfield, D., Abisla, R., Bunescu, V., Chiranov, M., Garroux, C., Maister, A., González Martín, L., Paley, J., and Rae-Scott, S. (2019). Innovative impact planning and assessment through global libraries: Sustaining innovation during a time of transition. *Performance Measurement and Metrics*, 20(2), 74–84. https://doi.org/10.1108/PMM-03-2019-0010.

Zaugg, H. (2015). Using a library impact map to assist strategic planning in academic libraries. *Library Leadership and Management*, 29(3), 1–17.

Zaugg, H. (2018). Begin again. In M. Britto and K. Kinsley (Eds.), *Academic libraries and the academy: Strategies and approaches to demonstrate your value, impact, and return on investment*. American Library Association.

Zaugg, H. (2020). The development, design, and implementation of a library assessment framework. *Journal of Library Administration*, 60(8), 909–24.

Zaugg, H., McKeen, Q., Hill, B., and Black, B. (2017). Conducting and using an academic library data inventory. *Technical Services Quarterly*, 34(1), 1–12. https://scholarsarchive.byu.edu/facpub/1809.

Zaugg, H., and Rackham, S. (2016). Identification and development of patron personas for an academic library. *Performance Measurement and Metrics*, 17(2), 124–33.

Zaugg, H., and Ziegenfuss, D. H. (2018). Comparison of personas between two academic libraries. *Performance Measurement and Metrics*, 19(3), 142–52.

CHAPTER TWO

~

Service Assessments

Holt Zaugg

Library services are the connections and interactions that enable patrons to use more fully everything the library offers, including resources, spaces, and personnel relationships (Beile et al., 2020). To be clear, library services are not the resources, spaces, and personnel relationships themselves but the interactions, either with a library employee or online, that facilitate the use of the library's offerings. Often these services extend the library's reach within (inward-facing) and beyond the walls of the library (outward-facing) to assist patrons in their learning and research.

Inward-facing Services

Inward-facing services refer to the services library employees provide for one another to help them complete their job requirements, plan for future services or service changes, and assist in decision-making. These services cross units, departments, and divisions within the library and result in better communication and interactions among library employees. Inward-facing services also facilitate better strategic planning and decision-making, which typically result in better outward-facing services. Some inward-facing services include:

- library IT support for collecting or accessing reports and data
- acquisition of library materials, including special collections archives that will be placed in the library's catalog
- library human-resources services for hiring and providing employment services
- facilities maintenance and development to improve spaces within the library
- collaboration among similar services (e.g., reference desks, subject-librarian consultations) to provide consistent and high-quality service
- process flow charts
- library security interactions, policies, and procedures
- library assessments

Many of these inward-facing service assessments view the value of library services in financial terms, as described by Malapela and De Jager (2018). The assessments help the library units indicate the value of either having their service within the library or paying someone else to provide the service for the library. The assessments help to indicate a return of investment funds for services used and delivered in addition to identifying ways that service delivery may be streamlined and improved.

Outward-facing Services

Outward-facing services connect directly to library patrons and focus on their experience. These services support student learning and faculty research activities as library employees share their knowledge about finding and accessing critical resources. Some outward-facing services include:

- reference or help desks, where patrons receive help as requested
- library instruction classes that help patrons learn how to access and evaluate different types of resources
- research and writing centers that help students find resources and write papers
- special collections materials that provide patrons the opportunity to examine and use primary sources for research and learning
- chat lines that provide quick online help to patrons

- subject-librarian consultations that provide one-on-one help with learning and research activities
- online media-instruction that helps patrons learn how to use a variety of tools
- reservation of group study rooms so groups of students have a space to work on learning projects
- interlibrary loan to access research and learning materials not found in the library but that are available in other libraries
- course reserve to provide quick, but limited, access to learning materials for all students within a course
- holds and delivery of materials requested by students and faculty
- online access via a library website that provides a virtual library experience to access electronic resources (i.e., e-books, journal articles)
- access to finding and checking out materials, including floor maps to materials

While many of these outward-facing service assessments have a financial aspect, they also have a social impact based on the interactions between library employees and patrons (Malapela and De Jager, 2018). Often these assessments are national assessments, such as LibQUAL$^{+®}$, MISO, and ITHAKA, that help librarians improve service quality by examining gaps between provided, perceived, and desired services (Ghaedi et al., 2020; Trivedi and Bhatt, 2019). The assessments may explore ways to standardize service delivery so there is greater consistency in how the library provides and maintains these services and how patrons discover and use the online or in-person services (Rennick, 2019).

Library services will vary because of university mandates and areas of focus, but whether services are inward- or outward-facing, their importance lies with the interaction between library employees and patrons or among library employees. The diversity of all library services indicates that there is not a one-size-fits-all assessment solution or plan. This section discusses some considerations to keep in mind when conducting assessments of library services by using the four assessment tasks outlined in chapter 1.

Design

With all assessments, design starts with framing the questions that need to be answered. For service points that offer a wide range of services, these questions may be quite complicated. Rather than conducting one large assessment, it may be better to split the assessment questions into more specific questions and conduct a series of small assessments that address each question rather than conducting one large assessment. These "bite-sized" assessments enable library employees to focus on a specific aspect of service delivery and note where one service may overlap with another. Smaller assessments may also focus on specific points in time. For example, different patron-librarian interactions occur at the circulation desk at the start of the semester when new students are setting up accounts and using the library for the first time as opposed to interactions that occur toward the end of the semester when patrons are seeking access to resources. More focused assessment questions also help determine when and for how long an assessment should occur.

As library service assessments examine ongoing interactions, there will be some intrusion on library patrons, similar to a third person listening in on a conversation of which they are not a part. Care should be taken that patrons using services are informed of the assessment and are not discouraged from using the services. Data, such as demographic identifiers, that can be collected without influencing patron interaction at a service point is preferred. The key is to provide open, informed consent to patrons, typically through a request to participate or other means to inform them that data is being collected to improve the service.

Interactions should also occur at the patrons' level of understanding. Library employees involved in inward-facing service assessments may understand jargon, acronyms, and discipline-specific terminology, but library patrons may find this terminology confusing. Terminology may need to be explained or changed when serving patrons. Additionally, it is equally important to see the interaction from the perspective of patrons using the service and employees providing the service.

An additional design consideration is whether to obtain an institutional review board (IRB) approval for the assessment. The IRB process provides a second look at assessments to ensure participants' rights and privacy are protected. IRB approval is typically needed only if the data will be disseminated beyond the library and university, but IRB protocols should be followed to protect both the participants and the institution, especially if assessments include elements such as deception (e.g., secret shoppers).

Data Collection

Whether at a single academic library or an assessment of all national libraries, data collection should include a variety of groups, including the different groups of patrons and those who work in the library. Each group offers a varying perspective that helps to create a more complete picture of what does and does not work (Anna and Srirahayu, 2020). While any given assessment may focus on one group over another, evaluators should seek to better understand how things work from all perspectives.

There are four types of assessment tools that are uniquely suited to examining service interactions: observations, video or audio recordings, surveys, and interviews or focus groups.

Observations

Observations allow an evaluator to watch, and, where possible, listen, to employee-participant interactions. Observations provide a first-hand perspective on interactions that are often recorded through field notes. However, conducting observations can be difficult if there is more than one service point, which is the case at most circulation desks and large libraries. The evaluator may miss part of the interaction when taking field notes or may not be able to hear the conversation. Observations also take a considerable amount of time and the evaluator may not be able to blend unnoticed into the background.

Video or Audio Recordings

Video or audio recordings provide an accurate record of an interaction that can be reviewed several times. However, participants must be informed that they are being recorded and participants' identity protected, whether they are library patrons or employees. Periodic checks of the recordings are also necessary to ensure that images and sounds are captured and to ensure that ambient noise or low volume do not adversely affect data collection.

Surveys

There are many types of surveys and several ways to administer them that are both unobtrusive and simple, ranging from short exit surveys conducted on an iPad to survey links sent in an email participation request. Employees at service points may also invite patrons to participate in a service survey, by using a slip of paper that briefly explains the assessment and includes a link or QR code connecting to the survey. If patrons are required to use a library card to access the service, surveys may not need to collect demographic and contact information as it may be collected automatically. In other assessments, a broader sample of all students may be surveyed to help evaluators determine how many patrons have used the library and are aware of the service. Contact information for students may be provided by the university registrar with the understanding that it will be used carefully and sparingly.

For example, a science and engineering help desk conducted a quick survey for patrons who used the help desk. After patrons were served, desk employees invited patrons to fill out a survey about their experience either using an iPad near the help desk or by providing a small piece of paper that repeated the purpose and invitation of the service survey and had links to the online service survey. Automatic time stamps on survey responses helped determine patrons' experiences during peak and nonpeak hours on a variety of services. The survey enabled those in charge of the help desk to focus on ways service could improve patron's experiences. The survey took less than five minutes to complete and allowed patrons to complete it at a convenient time.

In other instances, evaluators may survey all or most academic libraries to see a broader perspective of what is happening. Anna and Srirahayu (2020) did this when they surveyed all 629 university libraries in Indonesia to determine the degree of virtual services. This broad survey examined the availability of virtual reference services (e.g., chat, social media, email) to determine how service delivery varied among state, private, and international universities. The study was able to determine baseline measures of virtual services that universities offer and the preferred use patterns of patrons. It also indicated outside influences, such as internet access, that influence the access to and use of these services. With this information, Indonesian university libraries knew where they were with an eye to where they want to be.

Interviews or Focus Groups

Patrons accessing a service may also be invited to participate in an interview or focus group. A quick interview may be conducted as patrons finish using the service or a longer interview may be conducted at another time and place. Focus groups may be effective for collecting data from large numbers of patrons or library employees. Service points would need to collect contact information either by asking for it directly or requiring the use of library cards that contain the information.

One example of a quick interview occurred after a library added a southern entrance to the library's northern entrance. Gate counts indicated a 25 percent rise in traffic, but there was no indication of what the patrons were doing in the library. Using an iPad to record the interview and mini chocolates as an incentive, an interviewer was positioned near each entrance at different times of the day in a way that did not stop the flow of people. As patrons entered, they were invited to answer two quick questions: 1) What is your major? and 2) What are you doing in the library today? Responses were recorded on the iPad for later analysis. The entire data collection per patron took less than thirty seconds and, for the cost of mini chocolates, evaluators found out what library services were being used by patrons. They also found out that about 11 percent of those entering the library were using it as a "hallway" to get to the other side of the building instead of walking around.

Data Analysis

Data analysis should follow prescribed quantitative and qualitative procedures, depending on the data-collection methods used. Appropriate assessment questions enable evaluators to analyze results by using specific demographic identifiers of library patrons, such as gender, university status, and college of major. The demographic identifiers should be directly related to the service.

One type of service assessment examines the gaps between desired and delivered assessments (Ghaedi et al., 2020; Trivedi and Bhatt, 2019). These assessments emphasize services that exceed or do not meet patron expectations. Using this data, librarians can further examine what is or is not working well and why.

Dissemination

If data is collected on a regular basis, dashboards may be used by library employees to explore key components, such as the date and time of the interaction, the purpose of the interaction, and other pertinent factors. As with any assessment, a summary report should be written and shared with all stakeholders, as well as with other library employees who may learn from the assessment for service improvement and designing their own assessments. Where possible and appropriate, data should also be disseminated in publications and conference presentations.

Service Value and Decision-Making

Hogan and Hutson (2018) emphasize the importance of identifying what data the library is collecting and how this data is used to describe the library's value and assist in decision-making. Oakleaf (2012) formalized this process with a library impact map, which indicates where data is collected and how it is used, but other methods, such as data inventories (Zaugg et al., 2017), also provide information that indicates what, where, and how data is collected, and who collects it.

Some data is easily collected in an automated, routine manner but only offers superficial insights that can still be helpful in decision-making. For example, a dramatic drop in usage of a library chat line allows librarians to examine whether the service is worth continuing. Conversely, increased use of a research and writing center that helps students learn how to research resources and outline essays for class assignments informs the decision to expand the service. In both examples, the volume of use is important but is not the sole data source that describes value or informs decisions.

Service assessments should be both formative and summative. Formative assessments comprise a repeating cycle of assessments that assist in continuous adjustments to improve a service (Hogan and Hutson, 2018). Summative assessments help employees identify services that are well used or no longer needed. The use of formative and summative assessments ensures that library services are updated and relevant for student learning and university research activities (Ragon, 2019). Both formative assessments and summative assessments also help to describe value and facilitate better decision-making.

Summary

With a wide variety of services offered in libraries, no one tool or strategy will suffice to assess every service. Where possible, several data sources and tools should be used to give a more complete view of the service. Care should also be taken to develop an iterative assessment cycle geared specifically to inward- or outward-facing services. Doing so will help to determine the addition, deletion, or improvement of library services.

References

Anna, N. E. V., and Srirahayu, D. P. (2020). Evaluation of virtual reference and information services at university libraries in Indonesia. *Library Philosophy and Practice*, 1–10. https://digitalcommons.unl.edu/libphilprac/3583?utm_source=digitalcommons.unl.edu%2Flibphilprac%2F3583&utm_medium=PDF&utm_campaign=PDFCoverPages.

Beile, P., Choudhury, K., Mulvihill, R., and Wang, M. (2020). Aligning library assessment with institutional priorities: A study of student academic performance and use of five library services. *College and Research Libraries*, 81(3), 435–58.

Ghaedi, R., Valizadeh-Hagi, S., Ahmadi, E., Zeraatkar, Z., and Baghestani, A. R. (2020). Gaps between users' expectations and their perceptions on service quality of college libraries of Shahid Beheshti University of Medical Sciences: A case study. *Journal of Library and Information Technology*, 40(2), 131–36.

Hogan, S., and Hutson, J. (2018). Assessing access services: Building a five-year plan for sustainable assessment. *Journal of Access Services*, 15(2), 80–88.

Malapela, T., and De Jager, K. (2018). Theories of value and demonstrating their practical implementation in academic library services. *The Journal of Academic Librarianship, 44*(6), 775–780.

Oakleaf, M. (2012). *Academic library value: The impact starter kit.* American Library Association, 26–27.

Ragon, B. (2019). Alignment of library services with the research lifecycle. *Journal of the Medical Library Association, 107*(3), 384–93.

Rennick, B. (2019). Library services navigation: Improving the online user experience. *Information Technology and Libraries, 38*(1), 14–26.

Trivedi, D., and Bhatt, A. (2019). Quest for quality: Assessment of service quality of special academic institution library: Case study. *Performance Measurement and Metrics, 21*(1), 1–17.

Zaugg, H., McKeen, Q., Hill, B., and Black, B. (2017). Conducting and using an academic library data inventory. *Technical Services Quarterly, 34*(1), 1–12.

~

CHAPTER THREE

Case Study

Assessing Services and Staffing for Library Service Points

John S. Spencer, Foley Library, Gonzaga University

Changes in a library's environment, such as changes in staffing, services, or leadership, are often instrumental in moving an assessment project to the forefront. With a change in leadership and a new dean of the library at Gonzaga University, a vision for the future of the library was discussed in regular library staff meetings for consideration by the library as a whole. Prior to hiring a new dean, library leadership had implemented a learning commons model for the library building. Over a period of several years, the library building, known as Foley Center, was redesigned and renovated in order to provide space for student-centered services in the building. Building partners include the writing center, disability services, the center for teaching and advising, and information technology (IT) staff offices. An IT help desk and other services were incorporated in the building to engage students more effectively.

To improve library services, a new information desk was designed and constructed in close proximity to the building entrance in order to better serve library users. The new information desk replaced a traditional reference desk, which was the original service point when the building opened in 1992. In addition, an existing circulation desk provided services for checkout and reserves. Given the move to a one-desk model by other similar libraries, library leadership raised the question about whether two desks were essential in providing public services for circulation, reserves, information, and research support. A primary question for discussion by library leadership and the Public Services (PS) Department was: "How do we best provide current and any additional new services to the university community?"

Survey of Similar Libraries

To help librarians and library staff answer this question, other similar college and university libraries were surveyed to find out more about their service desks. The survey, conducted using SurveyMonkey, asked questions about library staffing for circulation, reference, and information services. Respondents (N = 22) reported that they had the following service points in their libraries: a) an information desk/kiosk (10 percent), b) a combined information/reference desk (10 percent), c) a separate reference desk (50 percent), and d) a separate circulation desk (60 percent). Some libraries (32 percent) had moved to a one-service-point model, providing information, reference, reserves, and circulation at one desk. These differences in service points were of great interest and required some further consideration.

The survey clarified that most libraries were open until 2:00 a.m. with staffing by library staff and student workers after 9:00 p.m. Another aspect of the survey was to find out more about specific responsibilities for librarians. A high percentage of librarians worked scheduled hours at an information/reference desk (75 percent). In addition, respondents said librarians frequently provided on-call assistance (75 percent), virtual reference (85 percent), and consultations by appointment (100 percent). In addition, the survey clarified that librarians' work included a range of responsibilities, including creating online resources, presenting library instruction, or serving as embedded librarians to serving on library/university committees, as well an array of professional activities.

Assessment Task Force Created

With the survey providing some pathways for further exploration and discussion, library leadership recommended that a PS task force be formed to assess the current model for providing information and circulation desk services and staffing. While the current staffing for the information desk provided a high level of information and research support, it was also staff-intensive. Staffing required daily desk shifts by librarians, library staff, and student workers to manage the operation both during the regular work week and also on weekends and evenings. New roles for librarians and library staff were under consideration as part of developing a broader vision for the library's future. To consider some changes to staffing and services at the new information desk, the PS task force was charged with assessing the current operation with a focus on services and staffing. Renovations could be proposed if required for the development of a new model of service delivery, although funding would need to be secured at the campus level.

The task force brought together the author as the chair, two library staff members, and one librarian, all members of the PS Department. At that time, the PS Department consisted of four full-time librarians and two part-time adjunct librarians, as well as two full-time circulation and three interlibrary loan staff members. To bring about a better understanding of trends and changes in academic libraries, task force members did exploratory reading about the landscape for academic libraries in the twenty-first century.

Current trends indicate that academic libraries are operating in an environment where digital publishing and technology are ubiquitous. The book *Reimagining the Academic Library* (Lewis, 2016) was a key text for understanding how technology innovations, such as the world wide web, have dramatically changed academic library services and staffing requirements. In order to consolidate their role in the academic arena, Lewis (2016) recommended that academic libraries look for ways to adopt new technologies that appeal to undergraduates who tend to be early adopters of the latest ways to use technology.

One of the first goals of the task force was to review the library's current services and staffing operations. Task force members identified specific services at the circulation and information desks and added them to a Google document so all task force members could contribute to building a comprehensive list. Observations of library employees serving library users validated these services and added additional services to the list. The next step was to "classify" the desk services, clustering them in categories: information, reference, circulation, reserves, printing, technology, study rooms, and so on. This classification process was familiar to task force members, helping the group better understand the differences and similarities of the services provided at the circulation/reserves and the information/reference desks.

Generation Z as Library Users

Given that undergraduate students are the primary users of the library's service desks, the task force wanted to find out more about the current generation of students entering college directly from high school. Most undergraduates attending college are part of Generation Z, born between the mid-1990s to early 2000s. Gen Z makes up about a quarter of the U.S. population and outnumbers millennials and baby boomers (Dill, 2015). According to most research, Generation Z students are considered "digital natives," who are tech-savvy and prefer online access to information as their first choice. Gen Z students are known as intrapersonal and social learners, which means they not only like to work independently but also enjoy interacting in groups (Seemiller and Grace, 2016). In terms of library use, Seemiller and Grace (2016) assert that Gen Z students found libraries to be conducive to learning by providing resources and multiple interactive learning options.

Takeaways for the task force were that the library needs to focus on having a tech-friendly environment that allows for both independent users and group interaction. Students will be more inclined to use the service points for essential assistance with services in the building, such as finding specific resources, checking out materials, or getting help with library technology. Online services, such as providing virtual reference 24/7, are essential for students who like to engage from their dorms, home, or elsewhere. Access to online resources for student research is essential for the library, in addition to providing rapid interlibrary loans and personal research assistance from librarians either via online chat or appointments via Zoom.

One-desk Model

Using information gleaned from the initial survey of similar libraries, the task force decided to find out more about libraries that had a one-desk model. Library leadership was particularly interested in how to refine or reduce staffing and improve service delivery. With both an information/reference desk and a circulation/reserves desk, library staff were often fielding similar questions or referring library users to the other desk for specific services. Libraries that were surveyed provided some details about their staffing. A tiered staffing model was employed by 50 percent of the libraries surveyed with both librarians and library staff working at the service points, along with student employees. For library administration, moving to a one-desk model provided a way to give librarians and library staff more time to pursue other responsibilities away from the service desks.

Libraries that had the one-desk model were contacted via email to set up an interview with a member of the task force. A range of questions were asked about the way the desk was staffed: What does the one-desk model look like at your library? How is it implemented? Can you provide a photo of the physical space? Overall, libraries with a one-desk model had librarians "on-call," while library staff and student employees were the ones staffing the desk. Using a triage approach, quick informational questions were answered at the desk and more extensive research questions were referred to the on-call librarian.

Design Thinking

In exploring ways to improve the user experience (UX) at the service desks, the task force utilized the process of design thinking. The work of Stephen Bell, a librarian at Tulane University, was recommended by library leadership. To address the many challenges facing academic libraries, such as improving service delivery, Bell believes design thinking is "based on the premise of correctly identifying the problem before developing solutions" (Bell, 2010, p. 4). For our team, that meant clarifying and understanding the problems related to the service desks that require solutions. One problem related to the UX for library users who may not be familiar with the library service desks. Both service points are near the library's front entrance. Patrons often ask questions at one desk, only to be referred to the other desk. In addition, having two desks presents an ongoing challenge with staffing. Library staff and student employees work at both desks covering most hours that the library is open. Cross-training is an ongoing process for new student employees, given that different skills and knowledge are needed for working at each desk.

Using design thinking principles, Bell undertook a wide range of challenges, such as open educational resources (OER) initiatives, UX for academic libraries, office ecosystems, and library website redesign. According to Bell (2018), libraries can benefit by applying design thinking to improve the UX. Using the principles of design thinking and keeping a focus on the UX was an impetus to ask key questions. Bell recommends that teams determine "how to address the gap between the service in its current state and what would be required to improve the user experience" (Bell, 2018, p. 5).

After reviewing Bell's ideas, the task force discussed ways to improve service at each desk and analyzed what that would mean for staffing. The team also looked at how library users engage with the library at the service desks and considered if a one-desk model would improve services. This is what Bell described as approaching the service as a user, in order to improve students' UX. In a literature review of how UX has influenced libraries in the twenty-first century, Bell clarifies that it is not necessary to design for a specific experience, but rather design for an environment that will "make it possible for any users to derive satisfaction from his or her personal experience" (Bell, 2014, p. 373). With a better understanding of UX and design thinking, the task force developed some recommendations for service delivery and staffing at the service desk(s).

Recommendations

The task force recommended that moving from two service desks to a one-desk model would be ideal for refining staffing and improving services, while reducing the need for staffing and managing two desks. By moving the services to one desk, supervision would be easier for library staff who have offices behind the circulation/reserves desk. A one-desk model provides a way to handle services seamlessly, whether students need information or research assistance or want to check out books or reserves. This model requires some renovation of the service desks and the adjacent space for staff workspaces. A related recommendation was to make use of the existing information desk for a self-checkout station.

Ideally, there would be a colocation of services for information, research support, circulation, and reserves. Since the desk is a way for students to get immediate assistance, librarians would be scheduled for "on-call" research assistance. Librarians can work in their offices and be logged in to the library's online chat service to field informational or research questions while on-call. If a student needs help, she or he can either meet with a librarian right away or schedule an appointment for a later time. In reviewing how other libraries changed their service desks, it was clear that libraries consistently provide "on-call" and "off-desk" services, such as consultations with librarians who provide immediate or scheduled research assistance.

Based on what other libraries are doing, the task force recommended that most of the services at the one desk be provided by student employees. The recommendation is that all public services staff and student employees are part of the same team. Team leaders can work with students during the daytime, evenings, and on weekends. Typically, library staff work until 9:00 p.m. in the evenings, and then student employees provide basic services until the library closes at 2:00 a.m. The new model recognizes that student employees are trained to provide basic levels of assistance and can refer users to their team leader, library staff, or librarians for additional assistance.

Student employees are trained to respond to most questions about technology and printing requests. Currently they know how to make referrals to the IT help desk or library staff as needed. Based on what was learned from other libraries, the library's services should emphasize supporting library-related technology. This means training student employees on how to respond to questions about logging in to library resources, how to use the campus network and printing services, and when to defer to their team leader or supervisor if needed. Referrals to the university's IT Department are easy, with an IT help desk on the library's lower level and a tech bar in the student center adjacent to the library.

In keeping with a new model for service, a new name, User Services, was proposed. A list of possible names for the PS Department was reviewed, after surveying similar libraries. Details on the services at the one-desk were determined to be the following, generally:

- responding to walk-up users or phone calls
- answer questions about library resources
- check out books/materials/reserves and consider self-check out in the future
- information/directional and quick reference questions
- assist with periodicals and interlibrary loan
- referral to an on-call librarian for research assistance
- assist with library technology and printing/scanning/copying

After the task force finalized their recommendations, changes took place over a period of time. Library leadership implemented ways to refine the staffing at the two service desks. Library student employees were trained to provide services at the information desk. The circulation desk remained a service point for check out and reserves until a renovation could be implemented at a future time. Staffing for both desks is primarily student employees and also library staff or adjunct librarians for back-up and supervision. A department name change to User Services signaled a new direction. Also, a new library staff position was developed for a head of User Services, who is responsible for managing the staff and services provided at the information desk, circulation/reserves, interlibrary loan, and document delivery. The department includes five full-time library staff, two adjunct librarians, and ten to fifteen part-time student employees who work different shifts throughout the day and evening, including weekends.

Summary

Overall, the task force recommendations were well-received by library leadership. Using a multifaceted approach for the assessment of services and staffing, the library task force found that reviewing public services staffing and services at other libraries was essential to assess the broader library landscape. A key to getting off to a good start was to initially survey other libraries so task force members were able to consider a number of realistic options as they moved forward. By considering Generation Z as the primary library users, an emphasis on chat reference services provided a better way to respond to immediate questions from students who are primarily "digital natives." An understanding of UX and design-thinking principles provided a framework for thinking about current services and considering ways to improve the UX. Although a one-desk model was not an immediate outcome, the task force outlined specific recommendations for the future to renovate the space and provide one service desk with accompanying staff offices. In addition to making a presentation at a library staff meeting, a summary of the task force's written recommendations, as well as photographs of libraries with one-desk models in place, were also provided to library leadership to assist with future redesign and possible renovations.

References

Bell, S. J. (2010, March 2). *"Design thinking" and higher education.* Inside Higher Ed. https://www.insidehighered.com/views/2010/03/02/design-thinking-and-higher -education.

Bell, S. J. (2014). Staying true to the core: Designing the future academic library experience. *Portal: Libraries and the Academy, 14*(3), 369–82.

Bell, S. J. (2018, July/August). Design thinking + user experience = better-designed libraries. *Information Outlook, 22*(4), 4–6. https://hcommons.org/deposits/item/ hc:20851/.

Dill, K. (2015, November 6). *7 things employers should know about Generation Z.* Forbes. https://www.forbes.com/sites/kathryndill/2015/11/06/7-things-employers -should-know-about-the-gen-z-workforce/#4e0d4c9afad7.

Lewis, D. W. (2016). *Reimagining the academic library.* Rowman and Littlefield.

Seemiller, C., and Grace, M. (2016). *Generation Z goes to college.* Jossey-Bass.

Additional Resources

Additional resources, not cited in this chapter, are recommended for further exploration.

Bell, S. J. (2007). *On libraries . . . from Steven B.* Retrieved 1 September 2020, from https://sites.temple.edu/stevenb/.

Library. 2018. (2018, March 8). Design thinking for libraries. Online conference presentation recordings. https://www.library20.com/page/design-thinking.

~

CHAPTER FOUR

Learning from Our Users

A Usability Study of a Library Website

Susan E. Montgomery, Rollins College

The academic library website also serves as the main gateway for users to access an array resources provided specifically to meet their learning and research needs. The website is both a virtual space and a library service that users must be able to easily access and navigate the website to obtain content. This chapter focused on the website as a service.

To understand how library users navigate the website, librarians conduct usability testing. In general, usability testing is a method often administered by an organization to determine if users are able to use a product and understand what the challenges are to using the product (Chisman et al., 1999). A well-designed, intuitive library website "reduces the cognitive load on user," enabling them to locate and access information (Detlor and Lewis, 2006, p. 251). This chapter discusses a usability study conducted on an academic library website and what was learned as users navigated the virtual site.

Academic librarians have actively contributed to the research conversation regarding website usability since the early 2000s. The proliferation of websites during the 1990s sparked an interest to gain insight from library users about their experience with the website (Gallant and Wright, 2014). Emanuel (2013) stressed the importance of collecting various forms of data—both qualitative and quantitative—in usability research, as both contribute unique knowledge and feedback. As noted by Bergart and McLaughlin (2020), "qualitative research explains, discovers, and generates new ideas while quantitative research measures and validates existing things" (p. 3). Researchers at Northern Illinois University determined that qualitative data gathered during their usability study provided more insight about the short-comings and benefits of their website than quantitative data (VandeCreek, 2005). At Valdosta State University, librarians included focus groups and questionnaires during their website usability test, indicating a preference for qualitative data (Gallant and Wright, 2014).

The participant pool for a library website usability study can vary depending on the institution and the goals for the study. Three user groups that are often included to participate in a study are faculty, students, and staff. These groups are composed of diverse constituents who provide a unique perspective. Researchers specify who to include in the usability study based on the purpose and the research question they seek to answer. At the University of Buffalo, researchers selected undergraduate students for the focus of their usability study (Battleson et al., 2001). A usability study at Florida International University included faculty and students who completed identical tasks to provide researchers comparative quantitative and qualitative data (Hammill, 2003).

After data collection is completed, researchers analyze the data to draw conclusions and propose modifications to the website. Website usability studies reveal interesting details and insights about how users seek information with the goal to improve the overall user experience. For this usability study, the research team gathered and analyzed data to ascertain what users do well on the library website and what they find challenging. Both quantitative and qualitative data revealed usage patterns and identified what changes should be made to the website to help users access information more effectively.

Background

The Olin Library is the only library on the Rollins College campus, a small private college with approximately three thousand students. Rollins is com-posed of three schools: the College of Liberal Arts (CLA); the Hamilton Holt School (Holt), which offers evening and weekend undergraduate and graduate programs; and the Crummer School of Business, which includes an MBA program and a small doctorate program. In 2014, the library website was part of a campus-wide website transformation that included changes to the layout, color, font, and college logo. All departments revised their sites to correspond with the new design specifications, with regular updates to maintain accurate content. At the time of this study, there was no anticipation of or indication for a college website overhaul. The research team, three librarians, and the digital services specialist had an interest to conduct a website usability study to better understand how users navigate and locate information on the library website and determine ways to improve that experience.

This study was completed over a year and included three stages: planning, data collection and analysis, and reporting with recommendations. The central research questions guiding this project were: Can our users access the information they need via the Olin Library website? If so, how? Is website navigation efficient? Are users satisfied with their experience?

During the planning phase the goals for the project were discussed, including the potential participant pool, methods for capturing testing content, and securing Institutional Review Board (IRB) approval. Previous usability studies were reviewed to understand what tasks were assigned in similar contexts and to determine the ideal number of participants. It was determined that a small number of participants would reveal common problems on the website (Cockrell and Jayne, 2002). Protocols, procedures, and data organization structures were developed for the study, including the best technologies to incorporate.

Planning and Methods

The Olin Library website serves a diverse community with a range of patron-specific needs. Faculty, students, staff, and community members access the website for different research and information-seeking purposes using somewhat different methods. The college's largest and most research-driven stakeholders are students and faculty. The usability team specifically recruited faculty and students to determine if each group's searching needs were being met by the library's current website. To be as inclusive as possible, both CLA and Holt students were recruited. Any interested faculty members were invited to secure diverse faculty representation. Students represented the departments with the most majors: business and communication, as well as students from the Holt school, Greek life, and athletics. The team completed nine total usability study sessions: four faculty sessions (biology, sociology, health professions, and education) and five student sessions (three from Holt, two from CLA).

The Rollins IRB approved the study and the participants completed a Qualtrics survey consent form prior to the usability test and an in-person consent form at the time of their participation. Undergraduate students were asked to complete ten tasks and asked one follow-up, open-ended question (see table 4.1). Faculty were asked to complete eight tasks with a final follow-up, open-ended question (see table 4.1). This study based its structure on "task-oriented exercises," which center on "observing" the user's operation of the existing website (Cockrell and Jayne, 2002, p. 123).

To ensure anonymity, we removed participants' names when labeling each recording, and instead simply titled each video recording by participant type and number (e.g., Faculty 1, Student 1). The tasks were completed on Apple or PC laptop computers provided at the time of the study, depending on the user's preference. Open Broadcast Software (OBS) was installed to record the computer screen and the participants' navigation, including cursor movements, keystrokes, and any audio. Participants were encouraged to vocalize their steps and thoughts during the study. The Think Aloud protocol provided valuable insight on the participants' processes when completing assigned tasks (Hammill, 2003). Each usability study included a facilitator and a notetaker, along with the study participant. The facilitator read a prepared script informing the participant about the purpose of the study and the process (see appendix). The documentation, data gathered during the study, as well as the final report were uploaded to a password-protected site on the college's SharePoint server, only accessible by the research team.

Usability Tasks and Measures

Some benchmark indicators for each website task included having at least half of all test participants (50 percent) complete the task for it to be labeled achievable. Completion rates above 50 percent and less than 100 percent were labeled achievable with some barriers. A 100 percent completion rate indicated that participants could accomplish the task. However, further analysis was necessary to understand how users completed tasks and to suggest website changes.

Since faculty members and students use the library website to achieve unique tasks, with some overlap, tasks were particular to each group. Respondents were encouraged to explore the website as they completed their task. Tasks were developed based on past experiences with faculty and students and reflect critical library website functions that were considered typical and important for each group of stakeholders. For example, students tend to use the library website to locate materials for class (e.g., reserve or peer-reviewed materials required for a research paper). Faculty typically use the library website for pedagogical or research purposes. For instance, they may need to determine if the library has a specific journal title in their discipline for a class they are teaching or request an item via interlibrary loan for their research. These standard needs were considered when designing the usability tasks.

Table 4.1. Student and Faculty Website Usability Tasks

Usability Task	Tested Usability Activity
Student Tasks	
1. How do you get to the Olin Library website?*	Website discoverability
2. Use the library website to find a book on "cybercrime."	Simple search
3. Professor Kistler says she has a book on reserve for the course "LACS 200." How would you check to see if it is available in the Olin Library?	Course reserves
4. You need to find one peer-reviewed article for your research project on standardized testing in elementary schools. How would you do that using the Olin Library website?	Specialized/advanced search
5. Your professor recommended you use the database "PsycARTICLES" to locate relevant articles for your Intro to Psyc course. How would locate and access this resource via the Olin Library website?	Subject-specific database
6. Using the Olin Library website, how would you find out what time the library opens on Saturday?	Library hours
7. You want to ask an Olin Librarian a question, how would you contact one via the Olin Library website?*	Library chat widget
8. How would you schedule an appointment with a librarian using the library's website?	Schedule appointment with Librarian
9. Your history professor has asked you to use a primary source for your topic on the Civil Rights Movement, where would you go to find this type of material on the Olin Library website?	Primary source search
10. How would you find library collected resources for your Biology research project on the Olin Library website?*	Online research guides (LibGuides)
11. Was anything particularly challenging when using the library website to do these tasks? Was anything particularly easy?*	Participant's overall thoughts and level of website satisfaction
Faculty Tasks	
1. How do you get to the library website?*	Website discoverability
2. How would check to see what materials you currently have checked out from the library?	Personal library account access
3. How would you make a request to purchase a book or film on the Olin Library website?	Book purchase form/ policy
4. What if you were working with a student and needed immediate assistance from a librarian. How would you contact one using the website?*	Library chat widget
5. How would you find an individual journal that you use in your research using the Olin Library website?	Specialized article/ journal search
6. Where would you direct your students for quality academic sources on the Olin Library website?*	Online research guides (LibGuides)
7. Sometimes you are looking for items not in our collection, how would you request a book or article via Interlibrary Loan?	Interlibrary Loan access and process
8. Where would you first check to learn about any library resources or database outages on the library website?	Announcements
9. Was anything particularly challenging when using the library website to do these tasks?*	Participant's overall thoughts and level of website satisfaction

* indicates common tasks

Analysis

Each participant's session recording was analyzed according to three measures, effectiveness, efficiency, and satisfaction, to include both quantitative (effectiveness and efficiency) and qualitative (satisfaction) feedback measures to develop a full usability picture for the website (Barnum, 2011).

Effectiveness measured how many users successfully completed each task. Efficiency determined the average time taken to complete each task, the average number of clicks used, and the average number of excess clicks utilized (based on the minimum number of clicks required to complete each task). Each recording was divided into individual clips by task, allowing the viewer to count clicks and calculate the time to complete the task. Finally, comments made by the users about their feelings or thoughts while completing the tasks were compiled and analyzed for a measure of user satisfaction. Each researcher analyzed three recordings using each measure.

The committee developed a rank system to categorize findings. Website task results were rated as "good," "inadequate," or "unsuccessful" for students and faculty.

Good results are defined as:

a. There was 100 percent completion across all participants in the group.
b. The mean completion time was less than thirty seconds.
c. The average number of clicks used was equal to or only one click more than the minimum number of clicks required to accomplish that specific task.

Inadequate results are defined as:

a. There was above 50 percent but less than 100 percent completion rate for the participant group.
b. The mean completion time was more than thirty seconds but less than sixty seconds.
c. The average number of clicks used was only two clicks more than the minimum number of required clicks.

Unsuccessful results are defined as:

a. There was a less than 50 percent completion rate for the participant group.
b. The mean completion time was more than sixty seconds.

c. The average number of clicks used was three or more clicks above the minimum number of required clicks.

A detailed analysis of each task, organized by group, according to the three success measures utilized by team members is provided in tables 4.2 and 4.3. In addition, the tables include representative comments from test participants that reflect their satisfaction (or lack thereof) for each particular task or their responses to the open-ended questions asked at the end of each usability test session.

Student participants completed seven of their ten tasks with a 100 percent completion rate. The lowest completion rate was for finding and searching course reserves (80 percent) and locating primary source materials (60 percent). Overall, this shows a good deal of success with students' use of the Olin website.

Faculty participants completed only three of their eight tasks with a 100 percent completion rate. The lowest observed completion rates were for accessing their library account (25 percent) and locating the website announcements section (25 percent). Other challenging tasks for faculty included locating the book purchase request form (75 percent) and finding a leading academic journal in their field (80 percent).

Students and faculty accessed the library website with ease, and students located the library hours without problems (both 100 percent). Both user groups knew how to find a librarian when needed through the website—either via the chat widget, scheduling an appointment based on subject need, or knowing their library liaison contact (all 100 percent). Eighty percent of students were able to find online research help guides (LibGuides) created by a librarian, but one comment indicated that they were not "well-advertised." The majority of faculty users (75 percent) were also aware of these curated academic resources. Students were capable of both simple and advanced searches from the website (100 percent), although an advanced search did take significantly longer or required many more clicks. Furthermore, students found and utilized specialized databases with relative ease and efficiency (100 percent). Likewise, faculty were generally able to locate and use the interlibrary loan portal without issues, when given sufficient time (100 percent).

Incorporating three different evaluation measures for each task highlighted successful website functions and indicated areas of concern and challenges that users experienced when navigating the library website. For example, while locating a book in the library's collection had 100 percent completion rate for students, the mean length of time (55.2 seconds) indicated some students had difficulty completing this task. A correlation

Table 4.2. Student Data Task Analysis

Task	Effectiveness		Efficiency							Satisfaction Comments
	Completion Rate	Rating	Mean Time	Rating	Mean Clicks	Rating	Min. Clicks	Excess Clicks	Rating	
1*	100%	G	24	G	2.2	G	2	0.2	G	No comment
2	100%	G	55.2	I	4	G	3	1	G	No comment
3	80%	I	107	U	7	U	3	4	U	Just because I didn't have a space (e.g., LAC200 vs. LAC 200) the results didn't come up
4	100%	G	95.6	U	7.2	U	3	4.2	U	No comment
5	100%	G	41.6	I	4	G	3	1	G	Re: Using "Find Resources by Subjects" tab—It helps narrow it down especially when I'm looking for something for English for example, I'm not going to use something for Physics
6	100%	G	30.1	I	4	I	2	2	I	Calendar and hours should be moved to home page
7*	100%	G	28.6	G	2	G	1	1	G	No comment
8	100%	G	46.8	I	4	G	3	1	G	I've tried scheduling the appointment before but it's easier to just email [the librarian] I wasn't able to find a time that worked for me through the online scheduler but when I emailed [the librarian] he worked with me and we got a time together
9	60%	I	76	I	6.7	G	5	1.7	G	I'm wondering if they have something called "primary sources" here—while scrolling through the left-hand side menu bar in Primo results. I think there needs to be a tab for it.
10*	80%	I	78.5	I	4.5	G	4	0.5	G	Re: Research guides—these aren't really well advertised

G = Good, I = Inadequate, U = Unsuccessful. Min. = Minimum. Mean Time is in seconds. *Indicates identical or similar task tested for students and faculty participants (1 = 1, 7 = 4, and 10 = 6).

Table 4.3. Faculty Data Task Analysis

	Effectiveness				Efficiency					
Task	Completion Rate	Rating	Mean Time	Rating	Mean Clicks	Rating	Min. Clicks	Excess Clicks	Rating	Satisfaction Comments
1*	100%	G	29	G	2	G	2	0	G	No comment
2	25%	U	108.8	U	6	I	4	2	I	I have no idea where to do that. I can't complete this task. There should be a Circulation icon or something. Right now I'm annoyed I can't get to it. I usually just call Circulation.
3	75%	I	101.3	U	4	G	4	0	G	I used to get cards with book information to request but don't recall getting any this year. I would probably email my librarian.
4*	100%	G	39	I	2.3	G	3	4.2	I	I would call her or email her; if I use the chat feature, I don't know who will respond so I would prefer to contact the librarian directly. I'd call 'my librarian' directly.
5	75%	I	214	U	7	I	5	2	I	When searching within "Find Journal" for journal title and it is not in our collection—"There should be some message telling [the user] to request it via ILL."
6*	75%	I	81.7	U	5.3	I	2	2	I	No comment
7	100%	G	40.3	I	4.3	G	4	.25	G	No comment
8	25%	U	102	U	8	U	0	8	U	Faculty member never found announcements but mentioned that he thought "It would be best to have that information on the homepage . . . so that it would appear as a sort of alert for people." "Everything seems hard for me to get to."

G = Good, I = Inadequate, U = Unsuccessful. Min. = Minimum. Mean Time is in seconds. *Indicates identical or similar task tested for students and faculty participants (1 = 1, 7 = 4, and 10 = 6).

between the time spent on task and the student's academic background warrants further analysis. Similarly, students located the hours of operation for the library on a specific day of the week with 100 percent completion, but the average number of clicks (four) surpassed the minimum number of clicks by two. One student participant demonstrated a preference to use the library's Facebook page to complete this task. Additionally, faculty had 100 percent completion when contacting a librarian for immediate assistance, but the mean completion time (thirty-nine seconds) was higher than the research team expected. Further analysis revealed a hesitation by faculty members to make a quick decision. One faculty participant stated a preference to email the liaison librarian directly rather than using the chat tool feature prominently located on the library homepage, resulting in more time needed to complete the task.

Summary and Recommendations

This library website usability study revealed the need for changes in order to help users access information more effectively. The usability tasks helped reveal the challenges users encounter as well as the tasks they could complete with ease. Students successfully completed tasks, such as locating a book in the collection, finding a subject-specific database, and contacting a librarian, but the library website could improve access to course reserves. Faculty users were less successful and satisfied with the library website. They desired a more obvious location to access individual library accounts.

By analyzing each task using quantitative and qualitative measures, the research team identified unnoticed problem areas using the effectiveness, efficiency, and satisfaction ratings to evaluate each task for students and faculty. This method provided the research team with a more comprehensive and robust understanding of how users navigate the library website and accessed information.

Four website changes were proposed. First, rename the label "Overview" to "Home" to help users return to the library homepage. Second, the homepage menu should incorporate more user-oriented language based on their roles at the college (e.g., Faculty Resources, Student Resources, Community Resources). The website should emphasize the information-seeking activities of the user rather than the library services (Detlor and Lewis, 2006). Third, provide an FAQ option. Fourth, critical and time-sensitive content such as hours of operation and announcements should be more prominent on the homepage.

More specific and labeled navigation on the website for each user group would improve the user experience. After receiving the recommendations, the library's digital services specialist created mockups illustrating potential changes to the library homepage and navigation menu, which were shared with library employees with the goal of revising the website. Once modifications are incorporated, a subsequent usability study on the new site will be conducted with both faculty and student participants. As Battleson et al. (2001) reported, library users' needs are constantly changing, and the website must be maintained and designed to meet those changes (p. 196).

Acknowledgment

The author wishes to express her appreciation to the members of the Olin Library Usability Team for their time, support, and dedication to this study: Juan Gonzalez, Rachel Walton, and Maridath Wilson.

References

Barnum, C. M. (2011). *Usability testing essentials: Ready, set . . . test!* Morgan Kaufmann.

Battleson, B., Booth A., and Weintrop J. (2001). Usability testing of an academic library website: A case study. *The Journal of Academic Librarianship, 27*(3), 188–98.

Bergart, R., and McLaughlin J. (2020). Can user experience research be trusted? A study of the UX practitioner experience in academic libraries. *Weave: Journal of Library User Experience, 3*(2), 1–19.

Chisman, J., Diller K., and Walbridge, S. (1999). Usability testing: A case study. *College and Research Libraries, 60*(6), 552–69.

Cockrell, B. J., and Jayne, E. A. (2002). How do I find an article? Insights from a web usability study. *The Journal of Academic Librarianship, 28*(3), 122–32.

Detlor, B., and Lewis, V. (2006). Academic library web sites: Current practice and future directions. *The Journal of Academic Librarianship, 32*(3), 251–58.

Emanuel, J. (2013). Usability testing in libraries: Methods, limitations, and implications. *OCLC Systems and Services: International Digital Library Perspectives, 29*(4), 204–17.

Gallant, J. W., and Wright, L. B. (2014). Planning for iteration-focused user experience testing in an academic library. *Internet Reference Services Quarterly, 19*(1), 49–64.

Hammill, S. (2003). Usability testing at Florida International University Libraries: What we learned. *The Electronic Journal of Academic and Special Librarianship, 4*(1), 1–13.

VandeCreek, L. M. (2005). Usability analysis of Northern Illinois University Libraries' website: A case study. *OCLC Systems and Services, 21*(3), 181–92.

Appendix: Usability Test Script

Hi, PARTICIPANT NAME. My name is FACILITATOR NAME, and I'm going to be walking you through this session today.

[close door prompt]

[computer choice prompt]

Before we begin, I have some information for you, and I'm going to read it to make sure that I cover everything.

We asked you here today to help us learn how members of the Rollins community use the Olin Library website to find information and to get feedback on how we can improve it. The session should take approximately thirty minutes to complete.

We have installed software on this machine to record the steps you take when completing each task. My library colleague will be taking notes as you complete each task. These recordings will help us analyze how you use the website and will not be shared with anybody outside research team. Are you comfortable with this?

Now I need you to sign an assent form, which indicates that you agree to participate voluntarily in this study.

The first thing I want to make clear is that we're testing the *website*, not you. You can't do anything wrong here. In fact, this is probably the one place today where you don't have to worry about making mistakes.

As you use the site, I'm going to ask you as much as possible to think out loud: to say what you're thinking. This will be a big help to us. That is not a very natural thing to do, so sometimes I will prompt you.

Also, please don't worry that you're going to hurt our feelings. We're doing this to improve the site for all of our users, so we need to hear your honest reactions.

If you have any questions as we go along, just ask them. I may not be able to answer them right away, since we're interested in how people do when they don't have someone sitting next to them to help. But if you still have questions when we're done, I'll try to answer them then. If you need to take a break at any point, just let me know.

Do you have any questions so far?

Now I'm going to start the recording. [Facilitator starts recording on computer.]

Now I'm going to ask you to try doing some specific tasks. I'm going to hand you an index card with the task written on it. Please read each one out loud and complete the task.

And again, as much as possible, it will help us if you can try to think out loud as you go along.

[Hand the participant first index card and read it aloud. Allow the participant to proceed until the task is complete or the participant becomes frustrated.]

[If participant becomes frustrated, facilitator can suggest one possible route such as "Some users go . . ." or "You could try . . ."]

[Continue with subsequent index card, handing each one individually to the user and reading it out loud.]

[Confirm with participants that they are finished with a task by asking, "Do you think you've completed this task?"]

Tasks completed.

Thanks, that was very helpful.

Do you have any questions for me now that we're done?

Would you like to be notified about the results of this study?

[Facilitator stops recording, saves onto computer and USB.]

~

CHAPTER FIVE

Assessing and Evaluating the Maryland Shared Open Access Repository

Elizabeth Fields, Stevenson University Library

Joseph Koivisto, University of Maryland, College Park

Chuck Thomas, University System of Maryland and Affiliated Institutions Library Consortium

Institutional repositories (IR), or "digital collections capturing and preserving the intellectual output of a single or multi-university community" (Crow, 2002, p. 1), were first introduced to most academic libraries nearly two decades ago. U.S. and international advocacy groups promoted IRs as part of a strategy to reform existing scholarly communication systems. Today, IRs are commonly found in the service portfolios offered by academic libraries. They differ among institutions in their scope, policies, audiences, underlying technical platforms, content, and management. Assessing and evaluating any particular IR can be challenging because one-size-fits-all models do not work well. Despite this challenge, IR assessment is vital, as it can reveal useful insights into user relationships to open access resources, the reach and impact of institutionally produced scholarship, and returns on infrastructural investments.

Considering the challenges inherent in assessing and evaluating an IR for a single institution, one can imagine the complexities of evaluating an IR that serves multiple institutions and libraries. The Maryland Shared Open Access Repository (MD-SOAR) has operated since 2015 as an opt-in and jointly governed digital repository service for multiple institutions in Maryland. Sponsored by the USMAI Library Consortium, the MD-SOAR platform is available for use by both member and nonmember libraries in the state. It provides an affordable shared platform upon which libraries can build their own IR services and distribute openly accessible scholarly and creative works. Based on the open-source DSpace application, MD-SOAR is a multitenant implementation, supporting its ten member institutions via a single installation of the application.

In support of a recent request for continuing consortium support, MD-SOAR's shared governance group conducted an evaluation of the service. This chapter briefly reviews various literature-based approaches to IR assessment and explains how the MD-SOAR assessment was conducted, including a summary of findings, limitations of the methodology, lessons learned, and future actions.

Literature Review

The proliferation of IRs and participating communities has generated a rich body of supporting literature. This corpus documents the evolution of ideas about performance indicators to assess and evaluate IRs (e.g., Westell, 2006; Thomas, 2007; McDonald and Thomas, 2008; Cassella, 2010; Bruns and Inefuku, 2016). Some approaches have been more institutionally focused on metrics such as author participation patterns (Carr and Brody, 2007; Thomas and McDonald, 2007), while others focused on broader impacts such as scholarly citations of papers in openly accessible repositories (Ferreras-Fernandez et al., 2013).

The body of literature on evaluating IRs is extensive and ever-growing and cannot be summarized here. However, a theme that runs across the entire body of literature is that assessment is an iterative and essential activity in managing IRs. Assessment activities allow administrators to chart the growth of the IR in terms of resources and users, to collect data on impact via usage statistics, and to illustrate impact as a means of securing continuing support and funding. As IR audiences vary based on need and use, so do audiences for IR assessment metrics. Bruns and Inefuku (2016) note that university administrators, faculty, and students all require different types of assessment data in order to properly communicate the importance of the IR as a "key player" in the institution and the scholarly communications ecosystem.

Analytical measures take many forms, ranging from basic tallies of IR content to more complex comparative measures (e.g., users vs. new users; record page views vs. file downloads). One interesting thread central to many assessment strategies is "human interaction" (Obrien et al., 2016), a key attribute that filters out important IR usage from the noisy data that surrounds web platforms. The rise of altmetrics presents additional avenues of investigation for IR assessment including social-media sharing, Wikipedia citations, and social bookmarking (Konkiel and Scherer, 2013).

MD-SOAR Assessment Initiative

Background
MD-SOAR's shared governance committee assesses repository performance routinely and conducts more in-depth evaluations periodically as part of requests for continuing administrative and financial support. The first report covered operations from 2015–2017 and included basic usage statistics and qualitative survey responses from committee members. Over the next two years, the repository grew considerably. The second assessment and evaluation, the focus of this chapter, covered operations from 2017–2020. In order to fully understand the growth and performance of MD-SOAR, the committee included qualitative survey responses from all users and expanded the collection of quantitative statistics.

Evaluation Methodology

Qualitative Assessment
Qualitative assessment employed a usage survey distributed via Qualtrics. Committee members sent the survey link to members of their respective institutions using direct emails, administrator emails via an email list, a newsletter, social media, and other marketing avenues. The survey was also linked from MD-SOAR's homepage to capture responses from users unaffiliated with any institution. It included twenty-one multiple choice, Likert scale, and short-answer questions. A full list is provided in the appendix.

Quantitative Assessment
Quantitative assessment of MD-SOAR was complicated by limits of the underlying DSpace platform. First, numerous server-side sources must be accessed and analyzed to obtain an understanding of repository record holdings, platform access, and users. Second, there are known data-collection issues related to record downloads. Obrien et al. (2016) observed considerable gaps in Google Analytics (GA) data collection related to bitstream downloads, casting doubt on the reliability of certain usage data. Third, to provide relevant data to MD-SOAR member campuses, it is ideal that all quantitative datasets be divided into campus-specific counts, a task complicated by MD-SOAR's single-instance approach. The committee identified specific quantitative

metrics related to record data, user data, user behavior, and citation. Each of these metrics was measured over a three-year period and compared over time to illustrate platform and audience growth since the last assessment and renewal initiative.

For record data, basic information, such as total items, distinct authors, and item type, was collected by querying the application database and assessing record metadata extracted from DSpace. Record and user statistics illustrate the repository's growth over time, while the distinct genre counts illustrate diversity in repository holdings.

User data covered two distinct communities: registered MD-SOAR users who submit records, and end users of the web interface. Counting registered MD-SOAR users required a simple database query and some minor review based on email domain and registration year, providing individual campuses with a general estimate of users per campus. However, MD-SOAR's registration policy does not require the use of an institutional email address, meaning counts are approximate. End-user data was collected via GA, consisting of unique user counts, new user counts, user sessions, and geographic data for user location. User behavior data was collected both from GA and the DSpace Solr web interface. Page-view and end-user search data was collected from GA, omitting URLs for pages that might obfuscate meaningful data (e.g., password reset, administrative, user-registration pages). Record file downloads were collected by querying the MD-SOAR Solr interface. In order to provide summary statistics for campus-specific views and downloads, both GA and Solr data required considerable post processing in order to align identifiers and URLs with campus affiliation. Citation counts, based on MD-SOAR-generated DOIs, were collected by querying the Microsoft Academic APIs made available through the Project Academic Knowledge initiative.

Findings

Qualitative Assessment

A total of fifteen respondents from seven institutions filled out the survey. Nine respondents were librarians or library staff members directly involved in the administration of MD-SOAR. Six respondents were nonlibrary staff or faculty, campus administrators, and students.

The majority of respondents reported overall satisfaction with MD-SOAR but admitted accessing it only rarely, with "a few times a year" the most common response. Seven respondents had used MD-SOAR to find, read, or download items, with six reporting that it is "extremely easy" or "somewhat easy" to find items.

Respondents also provided examples of their success and difficulty in using the system. Two respondents wrote that they "wanted to read an article" or were "looking for a specific article" and were successful in doing so. Other comments addressed difficulty in using MD-SOAR, such as a respondent's experience with being unable to find an item because "I was looking for one version of an author's name, and it was under another version (one had the middle name, one didn't)."

Respondents were next asked if they had used MD-SOAR to upload items and, if so, how easy or difficult it was. Eight respondents uploaded items, with four reporting that it is "extremely easy" or "somewhat easy" to upload items. Respondents also had an opportunity to comment on requested features and their overall experiences (see table 5.1).

Quantitative Assessment

Quantitative data provided a broader picture of MD-SOAR usage, because it was not limited to respondents from specific institutions. Data was broken

Table 5.1. Overall Experiences with and Impressions of MD-SOAR

Respondent	Requested Features	Overall Experiences
A	"Single-sign on and staff submission form."	"Meets our needs and isn't difficult to manage."
B	"Author profiles would be very nice."	"It feels very clunky and ugly to use. I think there could be a lot of improvement on the user experience side with regards to accessing items in the repository. It's hard to sell it to faculty members when they see ResearchGate and Academia.edu as our competitors."
C	N/A	"Please create a box where first-time submitters must specify their institution. This will make it easier on administrators. I get an awful lot of emails from submitters who use their gmail [sic] or other personal accounts."
D	N/A	"I've never heard of this and am unsure what MD-SOAR even is"

down by academic year (AY). AY 20 was still in progress at the time of collection; therefore, data for the first six months of the year were included along with a projected count to give trends for the full year. The projected count was derived by doubling the number from the first half of the year, under the assumption that usage would be similar during the second half of the year.

Usage of MD-SOAR

Usage was assessed by examining the number of unique visitors, user sessions, page views, and geographic location (see figure 5.1). These three sets of statistics showed similar trends. The number of unique visitors, user sessions, and page views increased consistently each year, with numbers from AY 19 more than double those from AY 17 in all three categories.

User geographic location was collected by GA (see table 5.2). The majority of visitors were from the United States, which was expected given MD-SOAR's affiliation with Maryland institutions.

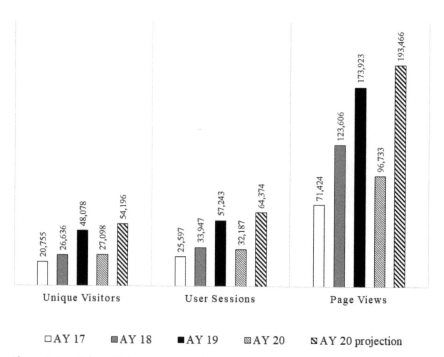

Figure 5.1.   Unique Visitors, User Sessions, and Page Views in MD-SOAR from AY 17 to AY 20. Fields, Koivisto, Thomas

Table 5.2. Unique Visitors from the United States from AY 17 to AY 20

Year	Unique Visitors		
	U.S.	Total	U.S. Percent of Total
AY 17	11,130	19,825	56.1%
AY 18	15,161	25,060	60.5%
AY 19	27,533	46,079	59.8%
AY 20	15,178	26,245	57.8%
AY 20*	30,356	52,490	57.8%

*AY 20 numbers and percentages are projected.

Content of MD-SOAR

Content was assessed by examining the number of records, authors, and citations of works, representing 14,407 total records and 9,964 authors (see figure 5.2). Approximately 21 percent of all records included two or more authors with an average of 1.44 authors per record, demonstrating the prevalence of collaboration between authors. Citation counts were obtained using Microsoft Academic, with 377 works being cited at least once. The most popular work was cited 554 times.

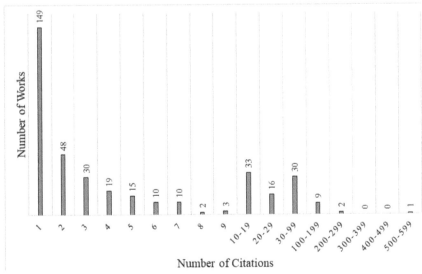

Figure 5.2. Number of Citations per Work. Fields, Koivisto, Thomas

Identified Limitations and Local Challenges

While the committee was generally satisfied with the amount and scope of the data, it encountered issues that illustrated the difficulties of assessing a shared institutional repository. For the qualitative assessment, the primary limitation was a low response rate, resulting in responses not being generalizable to the overall population.

Limitations on the collection of quantitative data were mainly a reflection of the tools used or technology in general. For example, GA counts unique visitors based on IP address, meaning that an individual who uses multiple devices to access MD-SOAR will be overrepresented. GA also uses browser settings to collect information about the geographic location of users. While this statistic is generally reliable, it does not account for users who have intentionally hidden or changed their browser settings through the use of anonymized browsing or VPNs. Furthermore, known issues related to the general reliability of GA data in evaluating IR usage and record downloads are a cause for concern. However, lacking an alternative methodology, evaluative approaches must operate within the confines of available data.

Solr data on the number of downloads from the repository included all bitstream accessions regardless of user, meaning that some of these downloaders may have been bot users or others might be considered systematic. As a result, individual human-initiated downloads and usage are likely lower than what was recorded.

Citation counts retrieved through Microsoft Academic are only available for indexed articles. Not all MD-SOAR records have been indexed; thus, Microsoft Academic is underreporting the number of works that have been cited. This discrepancy is most likely to be an issue with newer works that have not yet been indexed or would have a lower citation count due to their shorter availability.

Regarding these first three examples, there is no way to obtain more accurate data unless updates are made to GA, Solr, and Microsoft Academic, which would not be possible for the MD-SOAR committee members. The best way to address these limitations going forward is to use this report as a baseline and compare it with future usage, keeping the method of collection consistent.

The quantitative assessment was completed partway through AY 20, and, as a result, only six months' worth of data was available. Although the committee included full-year projections, they were not a substitute for exact numbers. Many factors, such as the academic calendar, research and grant cycles, and tenure and promotion schedules, influence the use of a resource throughout an academic year. In addition, the COVID-19 pandemic in 2020 had a profound impact on library services and could have led to either increased or decreased usage of MD-SOAR. Projections for a typical year would not account for this unusual situation.

Lessons Learned

The low response rate for the qualitative survey indicates the need for changes in the way committee members disseminate it. A comment from the student who had never used the IR and was "unsure what MD-SOAR even is" suggests that the survey did not reach the intended population(s). Because every respondent received the same survey, it is possible that the questions did not fit the way individual institutions and researchers are using MD-SOAR and potential respondents were disinclined to answer based on perceived lack of relevance.

Despite the small number of responses, the comments that were submitted were helpful. The reported difficulties in using the repository indicated that users find it more difficult to upload items than to search for them. Other comments provided insights for future enhancements to MD-SOAR, particularly authority control.

Soliciting responses from both librarians and end users was useful because it gave different populations an opportunity to describe their varying priorities. The comments illustrated frustrations on the parts of both populations, provided ideas for specific updates and changes that might improve the experience of using MD-SOAR, and underscored the fact that the IR needs to serve all types of users.

With regard to the quantitative assessment, the record, author, and citation counts were useful in the report. Assessment of the record counts illustrated the broad range of disciplines represented in MD-SOAR. The citation counts underlined the fact that researchers chose to cite works via MD-SOAR rather than publishers' websites, as well as works that are available only in MD-SOAR and not on other websites. These citation counts indicate that MD-SOAR fulfills its goal of making scholarship available when it would be otherwise inaccessible to the general public.

Future Actions

The expansion of the assessment strengthened the committee's presentation and report to the USMAI Library Consortium, which extended the service for another three-year period. As mentioned previously, the 2015–2017 report included minimal information. Broadening the scope of the 2017–2020 report illustrated that interest in and support for the repository had increased enough to warrant a more detailed picture. The committee emphasized the fact that usage had increased significantly since 2017. It did not have specific numeric goals for usage, so the numbers themselves were less important than the fact that there was evidence of consistent, substantial, and sustained growth. The committee should use the first two reports as a baseline for the next assessment report.

To mitigate the issue of a low response rate to the next qualitative assessment, the committee will look at alternative strategies of disseminating the survey. Contacting registered users from each institution might be effective in getting responses from users who are familiar with and actively using MD-SOAR. The committee should also consider employing more branching in future surveys so that respondents in certain demographic categories see questions specific to their usage of MD-SOAR.

Some responses to the qualitative survey suggested discrete actions that the committee plans to take ahead of the next report. For example, in response to the user comment about the format of the author's name, the committee began looking into adding the ORCID API for authority control. To support users who find uploading difficult, librarians should create instructional materials or assist in uploading documents.

Regarding the issue of projecting quantitative statistics for a full academic year, the committee will consider alternatives in the future. One option is to calculate the typical usage for each month of the academic year and base estimates on those calculations. Another option is to perform the assessment only when the full years' worth of statistics is available.

Finally, the committee should continually redefine what qualitative and quantitative data it collects as part of its reports. Because each institution uses MD-SOAR in slightly different ways, some may not need all the information being collected, while others may be interested in information that is not currently being collected. If a majority of committee members agree, questions and statistics should be replaced with more relevant ones, as necessary. Librarians involved in the assessment of a shared repository must continue to balance the priorities of all participating institutions while collecting and analyzing data as efficiently as possible.

Author Note

Joseph Koivisto: https://orcid.org/0000-0002-7515-2522.
Correspondence concerning this chapter should be addressed to Elizabeth Fields, Stevenson University, 1525 Greenspring Valley Road, Stevenson, MD 21153. Email: efields2@stevenson.edu.

References

Bruns, T., and Inefuku, H. W. (2016). Purposeful metrics: Matching institutional repository metrics to purpose and audience. In B. B. Callicott, D. Scherer, and A. Wesolek (Eds.), *Making institutional repositories work* (pp. 213–34). Purdue University Press.

Carr, L., and Brody, T. (2007). Size isn't everything: Sustainable repositories as evidenced by sustainable deposit profiles. *D-Lib Magazine, 13*(7/8). http://dx.doi.org/10.1045/july2007-carr.

Cassella, M. (2010). Institutional repositories: An internal and external perspective on the value of IRs for researchers' communities. *Liber Quarterly, 20*(2), 210–23.

Crow, R. (2002, August). The case for institutional repositories: A SPARC position paper. ARL bimonthly report 223. https://sparcopen.org/wp-content/uploads/2016/01/instrepo.pdf.

Ferreras-Fernández, T., Merlo-Vega, J. A., and García-Peñalvo, F. J. (2013). Impact of scientific content in open access institutional repositories: A case study of the repository Gredos. In F. J. García-Peñalvo (Ed.), Proceedings of the First International Conference on Technological Ecosystem for Enhancing Multiculturality (TEEM '13) (pp. 357–63). Association for Computing Machinery. https://doi.org/10.1145/2536536.2536590.

Konkiel, S., and Scherer, D. (2013). New opportunities for repositories in the age of altmetrics. *Bulletin of the Association of Information Science and Technology, 39*(4), 22–26. http://dx.doi.org/10.1002/bult.2013.1720390408.

McDonald, R. H., and Thomas, C. (2008). The case for standardized reporting and assessment requirements for institutional repositories. *Journal of Electronic Resources Librarianship, 20*(2), 101–9. http://dx.doi.org/10.1080/19411260802272743.

Obrien, P., Arlitsch, K., Sterman, L., Mixter, J., Wheeler, J., and Borda, S. (2016). Undercounting file downloads from institutional repositories. *Journal of Library Administration, 56*(7), 854–74. https://doi.org/10.1080/01930826.2016.1216224.

Thomas, C., and McDonald, R. H. (2007). Measuring and comparing participation patterns in digital repositories. *D-Lib Magazine, 13*(9/10). http://www.dlib.org/dlib/september07/mcdonald/09mcdonald.html.

Thomas, G. (2007). Evaluating the impact of the institutional repository, or positioning innovation between a rock and a hard place. *New Review of Information Networking, 13*(2), 133–46. http://dx.doi.org/10.1080/13614570802105992.

Westell, M. (2006). Institutional repositories: Proposed indicators of success. *Library Hi Tech, 24*(2), 211–26. https://doi.org/10.1108/07378830610669583.

Appendix: Qualitative Survey Questions

1. Are you affiliated with an MD-SOAR institution?
2. How would you describe your position?
3. How did you first hear about MD-SOAR?

4. How often do you access MD-SOAR?
5. Overall, how satisfied are you with MD-SOAR?
6. How easy do you find MD-SOAR to use?
7. Have you ever used MD-SOAR to find, read, view, or download an item?
8. How do you usually find items to read or view?
9. How easy is it to find an item that you're looking for?
10. Can you describe an instance when you were looking for an item and found it successfully?
11. Can you describe an instance when you were looking for an item and could not find it?
12. Once you've found an item, how helpful is the item's metadata in deciding whether you want to read it?
13. Have you ever used MD-SOAR to upload or submit an item?
14. How do you usually upload items?
15. If you upload items yourself, how easy is it to upload items?
16. How satisfied are you with the existing Access/Use/Copyright options in MD-SOAR?
17. Are you familiar with the existing OAI-PMH functionality in MD-SOAR?
18. Are you satisfied with the existing OAI-PMH functionality in MD-SOAR?
19. Would you be interested in seeing further systematic access or harvesting capabilities in MD-SOAR?
20. Are there any other features that you've seen in other repositories that you would like to see in MD-SOAR?
21. Is there anything else you'd like us to know about your experience with MD-SOAR?

CHAPTER SIX

Resources Assessments

Holt Zaugg

Traditional libraries, viewed as rows of books sprinkled with reading tables, are rapidly changing, as resources are now found online, in condensed storage, or on shelves. Library resources, everything the library has to lend, and access to those resources remain the reason libraries exist. However, student understanding of library resources is somewhat blurred because of technological changes. First, instead of just books and journals, libraries now have media resources (e.g., cameras, video recorders, audio recorders, and DVDs) available for checkout. Second, many resources that were previously only physical items owned by the library are now online, and while the library does not own them, it pays for access to them. Third, some special-collections items are digitized to increase access and prevent damage to the original items. Finally, the library either licenses or supports university licenses of online creativity and management tools.

Each of these changes alters how resource assessments may be undertaken as they typically involve other aspects of a library. For example, providing online access to electronic resources involves library services such as cataloging and website development. Additionally, resource development, maintenance, and evaluation are often affected by employees who have roles connected to resources. Collection development may require students and faculty to ensure that resources are needed and used, especially by patrons with disabilities (Kimura, 2018; Rysavy and Michalak, 2020; Sisler, 2020; Strong and Galbraith, 2018).

Resource assessments include determining how open educational resources for coursework affect student learning and library costs (Adedibu, 2008; George and Casey, 2020; Todorinova and Wilkinson, 2019) and how resources are cataloged and accessed. When the library collects a unique resource and then digitizes it, that item becomes both a physical and an online resource. Assessments may focus on which of these two resources are used more by patrons. Assessments of how acquired items are cataloged may vary by institution, and they may include assessments of how items are cataloged, such as passing all items through a central processing unit or decentralizing the process by using multiple librarians to catalog materials (Kim, 2018).

Other resources are not part of library collections but assist students with creative activities (e.g., Adobe), analytical activities (e.g., SPSS Statistics), or reference management tools (e.g., RefWorks, EndNote, Zotero, and Mendeley). The library provides access to or support of these resources to assist students with their learning and research activities (Speare, 2018). While the library may not own or physically have a particular resource, by providing access to and support of the resource, it becomes a library resource. This section discusses considerations when conducting assessments of library resources by using the four assessment tasks outlined in chapter 1.

Design

The design of resource assessments must focus on the aspect of the resource that is being examined and the purpose behind the assessment. Assessments typically focus on use patterns or cost-benefit analyses to ensure that libraries are getting good value for and use of the money spent on their resources. Other resource assessments focus on the types of resources the library has, collects, and provides for users. In these instances, consideration also needs to be given to the target population for the resources that are available and how they are used. Some assessments focus on collection development because subject librarians use students and faculty to help pick resources to development collections for which they are responsible (Strong and Galbraith, 2018). These types of assessments may also be used to indicate sensitive material or to ensure that resources can be used by patrons with disabilities (Rysavy and Michalak, 2020; Woods and Powell, 2019).

Another design concern is the physical location of different library aspects. For example, one library had a collection of DVDs and VCR movies housed behind a counter that was inaccessible to the general public. Several assessments were used as part of a prototype that resulted in most of this collection being moved from behind the counter to an open-access area where the movies were organized by genre and not catalog number. Assessments indicated that these changes were needed and helped to double circulation of the materials, but these changes also required assessments to determine how they affected space use and cataloging of the resources (Zaugg et al., 2020).

Resources also include tools students may use in their learning and research or just for fun, ranging from media equipment to online tools. These unique resources need assessments to help determine checkout policies and how library instruction assists patrons in the use of the online tools. Assessments also help determine if more or less of these resources are needed.

The diversity of resources may create challenges in how assessments are done. While most assessments of resources lean toward quantitative assessments, there is a time and place for qualitative assessments. Resource assessments are also heavily influenced by longitudinal data that helps to indicate trends and patterns.

Data Collection

Resource data is often automatically collected in logs that record what resources were used, who used them, how long they were used, or how funds were spent to build them. Using these logs, librarians can determine resource use patterns and cost-per-use without interrupting any patron (Howland et al., 2013). Other automated assessments may include pop-up surveys when students log on to public-access computers. These types of data collection are quick and involve little or no intrusion on patrons' activities.

Other resource assessments are more labor-intensive. One assessment that partnered with library services examined how quickly resources were reshelved for use by randomly choosing resources throughout the library and either placing them in return bins (in-house use) or checking them out and then returning them. The intent was to determine how long it took to reshelve resources for use. Twice a day, researchers checked to determine when the resource was reshelved for patron use. This assessment was repeated after a new employee took over the reshelving responsibilities to determine if new practices improved this rate of return.

There are four types of assessment tools that are uniquely suited to examining resources.

Use Logs

At the BYU Library, two separate assessments using automated logs indicated that only about half of all books added to the collection were checked out or used over a twenty-four-month and a twenty-year period (Howland et al., 2013; Strong and Galbraith, 2018). One of these assessments compared use rates from books added to the collection by normal means to use rates from books added from patron-driven suggestions (i.e., faculty orders, ILL requests, suggest-a-book requests, multiple-holds trigger, and ebooks). Results from using patron input to build collections indicated a better cost-per-use ratio and use rates that were three or more times higher than traditional collection-building choices (Howland et al., 2013).

Surveys

Surveys are typically used to gain further insights into how resources are used. Survey invitations may be sent via email to students who have checked out materials or use posters with a QR code or URL link. The key for these surveys is to focus on the specific resource so the correct data is collected that will answer questions for value description or making planning decisions.

Prototyping

While prototyping is a design tool, it is heavily connected with assessment, as a new process or resource is tried on a small scale, evaluated, and then adjusted for the cycle to repeat. In this sense, prototyping is an assessment tool that allows librarians to try out small changes to resource development, maintenance, or access before adopting them for all resources (Zaugg et al., 2020).

Focus Groups or Interviews

Where possible, students may be brought in for interviews or focus groups to help library employees understand their resource use or to request help with resource development. The intent is to delve deeper into resource use than simply using numbers to make decisions. Strong and Galbraith (2018) identified potential books that may be added to the collection, but before ordering the books, they asked focus groups of students to observe the book covers and details. Each person in the focus group rated how likely they were to use each book should it be added to the collection. The student ratings were compared with those of the subject librarian, causing the subject librarian to review his decisions and make changes in his collection-development orders.

Data Analysis

Data analysis is predominantly quantitative, as most data reflect numbers indicating amount, time of use, or cost. However, some qualitative assessments are possible with open-ended survey questions or interviews as described above. Appropriate procedures should be used.

Dissemination

Typically, reports of resources are only shared among library employees, but they may also be disseminated to other librarians via conference presentations and journal articles. The format for reports will vary from institution to institution, but reports should include sufficient description of how the data was obtained and analyzed as well as a brief summary of the findings and an indication of how the findings may impact library resources.

Summary

Resource assessments are valuable tools to ensure that libraries are using funds in frugal and appropriate ways to build collections and resources that are wanted, needed, and used by patrons. Most assessments lean toward quantitative data collection and analysis, but there is a place for qualitative assessments to inform how resources are used and how they may be improved. Because of resources' symbiotic relationship with library spaces and services, care needs to be taken to determine how resources impact other library aspects.

References

Adedibu, L. O. (2008). Catalogue use by science students in the University of Ilorin, Ilorin, Nigeria. *Libri, 58*(1), 58–62.

George, K. W., and Casey, A. M. (2020). Collaboration between library, faculty, and instructional design to increase all open educational resources for curriculum development and delivery. *Reference Librarian, 61*(2), 97–112.

Howland, J., Schroeder, R., and Wright, T. (2013). Brigham Young University's patron-driven acquisitions: Does it stand the test of time? In K. Bridges (Ed.), *Customer-based collection development: An overview* (first edition) (pp. 115–26). ALA Editions.

Kim, H. (2018). Two different institutional models in Canada: The University of Toronto libraries and the University of British Columbia library. *Journal of East Asian Libraries, 2018*(166), 1–4.

Kimura, A. K. (2018). Defining, evaluating, and achieving accessible library re-sources: A review of theories and methods. *Reference Services Review*, 46(3), 425–38.

Rysavy, M. D. T., and Michalak, R. (2020). Assessing the accessibility of library tools and services when you aren't an accessibility expert: Part 1. *Journal of Library Administration*, 60(1), 71–79.

Sisler, S. W. (2020). Optimizing discovery: Developing a holistic approach to man-aging a discovery service. *Serials Librarian*, 78(1–4), 69–73.

Speare, M. (2018). Graduate student use and non-use of reference and PDF man-agement software: An exploratory study. *Journal of Academic Librarianship*, 44(6), 762–74.

Strong, J., and Galbraith, Q. (2018). Letting the readers have a say: Crowd theory in collection development. *College and Research Libraries News*, 79(9), 502–4.

Todorinova, L., and Wilkinson, Z. T. (2019). Closing the loop: Students, academic libraries, and textbook affordability. *Journal of Academic Librarianship*, 45(3), 268–77.

Woods, A., and Powell, C. (2019). Sensitivity assessment of images collections. *Incite*, 40(11/12), 22–23.

Zaugg, H., Silva, E., Nelson, G. M., and Frasier, C. (2020). It looks a bit like this: Prototyping in an academic library. *Journal of Library Administration*, 60(2), 197–213.

~

CHAPTER SEVEN

Weeding Decisions for a Science and Engineering Print Collection

Gregory M. Nelson, Brigham Young University

Weeding as a Normal Workflow

Weeding should be a normal part of collection development. Librarians need to evaluate their collections and review how well those collections are meeting the mission of the institution. The more material that does not meet the needs of the patrons or support curricular demands of the university users, the more difficult it is for users to find and use the materials that do support their needs and programs. Unfortunately, no one has foolproof insight when an item is purchased of whether it will always be the best for patrons and the institution. A curricular focus today may be phased out by the university or merged with another campus unit in the future, thus an active collection evaluation is necessary. Unfortunately, evaluating a collection takes time, money, energy, and effort when other activities may be more interesting or pressing. It also takes some psychological resiliency to admit when purchasing decisions did not make the kind of impact one had anticipated (O'Neill, 2016). In some disciplines, materials may become outdated or superseded. Moreover, there is a finite amount of space in a library. Space for physical collections is not unlimited and becomes a valuable commodity when library priorities may outright change, adjust, or shift (Caminita and Herbert, 2016; Lee, 1993). One driving factor that spurred a complete evaluation of BYU's science and technology physical collection was a desire to repurpose existing space for other needs (Nelson et al., 2020).

Weeding Takes a Village

Weeding a large or small collection is a complex undertaking that should be data-driven. Ideally, a single subject selector should determine which data is the most appropriate to use for evaluating a collection, and, with contributions from others, make decisions about the disposition of that collection. That person bears the ultimate responsibility, authority, and ability to make final weeding decisions for a specific collection area. However, decisions should not be made in a vacuum, apart from secondary selectors, patrons, and other interested parties, especially from professors who may only occasionally use an item but nonetheless feel it may be a valuable and necessary component of their research and pedagogy.

An often overlooked but important aspect of evaluating a collection is to make sure that subject stakeholders are notified and allowed an opportunity to review the collection that is proposed for deselection or removal to onsite storage. This was evident when evaluating the medicine books found within the Library of Congress (LOC) classification system Class R, which encompasses a wide variety of disciplines. The primary selector for that collection benefited from feedback and input from several different librarians with subject expertise and assignments in those overlapping areas (table 7.1). The physiological sciences librarian at BYU has primary collection responsibility for the medicine area. She created initial lists of prospective items to be reviewed, completed the first evaluation of items found on the open shelves, and then invited librarians of related subjects to review the collection area before items were pulled from the open stacks and processed.

During the evaluation phase of the science and technology collection, the thoughts and opinions of the other library employees were sought and

Table 7.1. Subject Disciplines Associated With Medicine Within the LOC Class R

Biology	Nursing
Chemistry	Nutrition
Dietetics	Physiology
Medicine	Psychology
Microbiology	Sociology
Molecular Biology	

considered. Their feedback was often helpful and insightful. For example, the history librarian responded that he wanted to confirm that enough material was available for patrons on the plague in the Middle Ages. This topical area found in the medicine collection was infrequently used and would have been weeded differently had the timely advice from a colleague not been requested and communicated. This well-timed feedback from library employees was an important aspect of the project.

Selecting Metrics

The choice between what to keep, what to send to onsite storage, and what to discard is discussed frequently in collection development literature (Bowers et al., 2020; Burke and Kilb, 2019; Evans, 1987; Hawthorn, 1991; Snyder, 2014; Truett, 1990). Usage (checkouts or in-house use) of individual items is a common but important and easily measured metric for weeding decisions. However, usage should not be the only criteria that determines whether an individual item stays or is removed from the collection. During the collection-evaluation project, selectors determined how useful the following data provided by a subscription to OCLC's GreenGlass® tool would be as possible inclusion criteria (table 7.2).

Table 7.2. Data Available from OCLC's GreenGlass® for Weeding Decisions

Library Location	Number of Holdings Within
Recorded Use	Globally
Last Charge Date	United States
Publication Year	Comparator Libraries
Edition	ARL Libraries
Available in HathiTrust	Affiliated Consortiums
Choice® reviewed	Utah Libraries

Most of the criteria in table 7.2 were valuable for developing proposed exclusion lists, but some of the holdings' information, such as having a Choice reviewed item and access to a digital copy in HathiTrust, were less valuable. HathiTrust availability was a metric that was not used because so few items had been scanned into HathiTrust within the initial proposed deselection lists. The decision to not use it as a criterion was one based on practicality, which may be discipline-specific or change over time as more items are scanned and added to HathiTrust.

From the standpoint of how many items would be easily available through interlibrary loan, the most informative holdings data were at the U.S. level. It was decided that holdings in libraries at various other levels—globally, at ARL libraries, comparator libraries, Utah libraries, and consortia partners—were less important than the number of U.S. libraries that held an item. Selectors reasoned that interlibrary loan services within the United States would provide an acceptable timeframe for fulfilling item requests. Determining what the right number of U.S. libraries that had the item in their collection could be debated and was subject to the comfort level of each selector.

One Librarian's Weeding Criteria

The following illustrates how one librarian chose his or her collection-evaluation metrics. It is important that each selector apply the available metrics in a way that makes sense for the collections he or she is evaluating. The BYU Library valued the expertise of each librarian, his or her experience with the collection, and the current curricular focus of the institution, hence applying the same parameters for evaluation metrics was not mandated. The criteria that were developed for several collection areas were similar in some cases and quite different for others, depending on the subject expertise of the science and technology librarians and the needs of their assigned disciplines. For example, the chemical and life sciences librarian developed the following criteria for his assigned disciplines in microbiology, molecular biology, nutrition, dietetics, food science, chemistry, biochemistry, and chemical engineering. These criteria informed his decisions about which items to keep in the open stacks, which to relocate to an onsite storage facility, and which to withdraw from the collection. Lists were generated of candidates for weeding or long-term storage and did not include items that would be kept and did not need further evaluation.

Withdraw criteria:

- Library location: Publicly accessible on-shelf materials
- Recorded uses: Fewer than six
- Last charge date: No data or before 2008
- Publication year: Before 2008
- U.S. holdings: More than nine

Combined previous results with a list containing the following:

- Library location: Publicly accessible on-shelf materials
- Last used zero times on or before 2000
- Manually deleted publication date 2008–2018

The withdraw criteria resulted in the creation of a list of items that were on the open shelves, had not been used more than five times (in-house and checkout use), had no checkout data or had not been checked out after 2007, was published in 2007 or earlier, and was held in more than nine U.S. libraries. This list was combined with a second list that would identify anything on the open shelves that had no recorded use or had not been used since 1999, roughly eighteen years from the beginning of the project. This list also excluded all "new" materials published between 2008–2018, a ten-year timeframe from the start of the weeding project. The presumption was that those items had not had time to gather sufficient usage numbers and that the curricular focus was still appropriate to the needs of the university (Zuber, 2012).

There were some materials on the open shelves that did not get much use, but selectors did not want to remove from the library due to their potential rarity or loss to the library community. This chapter will not opine on whether these materials were not found in many libraries because they were rare and valuable or because they were rare and of poor quality.

Onsite Storage Criteria:

- Library location: Publicly accessible on-shelf materials
- Last charge date: No data or before 2000
- Publication year: before 2000
- U.S. holdings: Fewer than ten

Materials considered for this onsite storage list were any materials without checkout or in-house use or that had not been used after 2000, were published before 2000, and, importantly, were only available in nine or fewer U.S. libraries. Lists of prospective items for withdraw or long-term storage were generated for a subsequent in-person physical evaluation.

The Problem with Serials

In contrast to monographs, members of the department quickly found that monographic serials were an especially tricky set of items to evaluate in terms of selecting criteria. They learned that monograph serials might be listed in the library's Integrated Library System as individually cataloged items (fully analyzed) or they could be collectively listed on a single record (partially analyzed). A fully analyzed item usually had its own barcode and searchable chapter titles embedded in the record, while a partially analyzed item would typically only have the newest volume number added to the record without any additional information to differentiate it in the catalog from the previous volumes in the set. Usage or checkout information for partially analyzed serials is problematic as a weeding metric because usage is typically assigned to that serial's single record without the ability to differentiate checkout history at an item level. For example, a five-hundred-volume partially analyzed serial set with twenty-five uses might have twenty-five individual uses in twenty-five different volumes or twenty-five uses from the same volume. There is no way to determine which situation it might be. Further, in terms of holdings information, GreenGlass® may list that a serial is held in a library, but there is no way to ascertain quickly or easily how complete the serial set is from a holding library based on GreenGlass® holding numbers. A holding library may have one item, or five hundred items of a complete serial set. The GreenGlass® tool does not provide that information, and a librarian would need to search WorldCat to determine the breadth of the serial run. This was problematic when a selector's assessment relies, in part, on the number of U.S. holdings for an item or serial set. A good process is to evaluate serials separately from single monographs, and primarily rely upon subject expertise and the need to support the institution's current research focus and curricular needs. Usage numbers for serials are somewhat useful as long as the selector understands that those usage numbers have qualifications and limitations.

Lists and Streamlined Review

To simplify finding the location of the thousands of items identified in the lists on the open shelves, each item was physically tagged. A list for each LOC call number range was provided to our stacks manager, who then tasked student employees to tag each physical book on the list. This was a simple and easy visual cue for selectors to see where items that required review in the stacks were located. Student employees used purple painter's tape to tag books that were in the withdraw-review list and yellow tape for books in the onsite storage-review list.

Once a section of books was tagged in the open stacks, subject selectors evaluated the individual items with an eye toward the context, breadth, and depth of the collection topic and coverage. Much as a selector would use their personal expertise, judgment, experience, and knowledge to purchase materials for the collection, generating proposed lists followed by in-person review provided the opportunity for subject selectors to exercise those same skills to determine what should stay in the collection. There were many times in which items that were proposed for withdrawal were then identified as core components of a collection area. In those cases, it was easy to remove the painter's tape and place the book back on the shelf. Only purple and yellow tagged items were removed from the shelf after a selector's review and then moved to a staging and processing area. If a tag accidentally fell off an item prior to the item's removal from the open shelves, subject librarians did not worry too much, preferring to err on the conservative side and keep a book instead of removing one by accident. If a book with a purple or yellow tag was checked out during the evaluation process, the tag was removed upon reshelving and kept in the collection since the checkout was evidence of recent use. If an item slated for long-term storage was changed to withdrawal upon review, the yellow tag would be removed, and a purple tag added. The same would be done for an item planned for withdrawal was changed to long-term storage, the purple tag would be removed and replaced with a yellow tag.

Covering the Stakeholder Bases

Following each librarian's review, professorial faculty were invited to provide input on the materials that were proposed for withdrawal following the on-shelf evaluation. An online tool was developed in-house and linked to the library's discovery system and was crucial for buy-in from the faculty. This tool provided options for faculty to evaluate their primary subject areas or other areas of interest. An intuitive "vote to keep" button was placed within each electronic record for items proposed for withdraw coupled with a feedback feature that allowed faculty members to indicate why an item was important and should be kept. At the conclusion of the feedback period, library faculty responsible for the collection area received a report detailing each item that had received a vote to keep, its call number, the submitting faculty's name, home department, email address, and feedback comments. Faculty librarians evaluated each item and the associated feedback and then closed the loop with the professorial faculty member indicating the selector's decision. In nearly every case, the decision to withdraw an item was reversed and the item was kept in the library. In some cases, low-use items were placed in onsite storage. A decision was not reversed if an item was an unnecessary duplicate, an outdated edition with the newer edition already available, or significantly damaged. Damaged items were subsequently repaired or replaced and added back to the collection. Overall, faculty were satisfied with the process and the level of interaction and communication coming from the library. A forthcoming article will describe a qualitative assessment of the collection evaluation process with coded observations of success, failure, and improvements from the point of view of library employees and professorial faculty (Broadbent, personal communication, March 20, 2020).

Summary

Weeding is a multifaceted, sometimes frustrating activity, but it can result in a robust, effective, and focused collection. Choosing the "right" criteria for evaluating a collection should be defined by individual selectors based on the goals, aspirations, and curricular focus of each unique institution. Establishing easy-to-implement workflows when evaluating material in the stacks makes the task less like drudgery and more like an opportunity. When librarians work with each other as well as with their professorial colleagues, the process can encourage collaboration and a reassured patron base while achieving important goals associated with space and improved discovery.

References

Bowers, M., Allison, T., and Faltinek, A. (2020). Into the weeds: High-volume weeding at the Texas Tech University Health Sciences Center. *Technical Services Quarterly*, *37*(2), 120–27.

Burke, D., and Kilb, M. (2019). Managing a mass collections review from assessment to deselection. *Serials Librarian*, *76*(1–4), 123–29.

Caminita, C., and Herbert, A. (2016). The weeding planner—How a research library weeded approximately 2.76 miles of print materials from the shelves to repurpose library space or much ado about the new normal. *Against the Grain*, *28*(4), 11–21. https://doi.org/10.7771/2380-176x.7457.

Evans, C. B. (1987). Weeding the collection. In G. E. Evans (Ed.), *Developing library and information center collections: Library science text series* (second edition) (pp. 291–309). Libraries Unlimited.

Hawthorn, M. (1991). Survey selection and deselection: A survey of North American academic libraries. *Serials Librarian*, *21*(1), 29–45.

Lee, H. L. (1993). The library space problem, future demand, and collection control. *Library Resources and Technical Services*, *37*(2), 147–66.

Nelson, G. M., Goates, M. C., Pixton, D. S., Frost, M., and Broadbent, D. (2020). Collection weeding: Innovative processes and tools to ease the burden. *Journal of Academic Librarianship*, *46*(5) 1–13. https://doi.org/10.1016/j.acalib.2020.102139.

O'Neill, J. L. (2016). Weeding with ADDIE: Developing training for deselection at an academic library. *Reference and User Services Quarterly, 56*(2), 108–15. https://doi.org/10.5860/rusq.56n2.108.

Snyder, C. E. (2014). Data-driven deselection: Multiple point data using a decision support tool in an academic library. *Collection Management, 39*(1), 17–31. https://doi.org/10.1080/01462679.2013.866607.

Truett, C. (1990). Weeding and evaluating the reference collection: A study of policies and practices in academic and public libraries. *Reference Librarian, 13*(29), 53–68.

Zuber, P. (2012, June 10–13). *Weeding the collection: An analysis of motivations* (paper presentation). American Society for Engineering Education Annual Conference and Exposition, San Antonio, TX. https://doi.org/10.18260/1-2--22227.

~

CHAPTER EIGHT

A Playbook for Journal License Negotiations

Data-Informed Assessment

Berenika M. Webster, University of
Pittsburgh Library System

Keith G. Webster, Carnegie Mellon University Libraries

" . . . librarians have limited power. They also have no strong track record when it comes to negotiating. . . . That is their weakness and the publishers' strength." (Velterop, 2011)

A major function of any research library is to select and acquire information resources to meet the needs of its user communities. In 2019, the average expenditure on subscriptions by an ARL member library was around $10.2 million, representing over 75 percent of the total collections spent (ARL Statistics, 2019). This amount signals a significant investment by universities and requires librarians to secure the best possible value for their institutions. This chapter discusses data that librarians could assemble to inform their institutional journal license negotiations. It is hoped that much of the material presented here also can also be used in negotiations for other types of content and consortial agreements.

Over the past years, several changes have shaped the subscription negotiation landscape, including journal price increases that exceeded CPI (Bosch et al., 2020), the proliferation of big deal bundles of journal content, and a growing volume of free content available outside and inside journal subscriptions. Also, open-access publishing has become relevant to negotiations, as institutions seek agreements that provide both for readership and open-access authorship. Moreover, a growing adoption of preprint services and new forms of peer review put in question the idea of a traditional journal, with an increasing expectation that data, code, or other artifacts of the research process are published alongside the manuscript. These shifts inevitably have influenced the goals of libraries in journal license negotiations. While some seek to maintain their standard license with little change, many enter negotiations driven by a need to either reduce expenditure, unbundle Big Deals, or secure some quantity of open-access publishing rights alongside readership access to journals. To maximize success, librarians need to be armed with information about the relationship between their institutions and the broad publishing community, as well as highly granular data on their relations with the specific publisher under negotiation.

The Playbook

The shift from print to electronic journals has transformed the academic journal licensing business. In the print world, libraries typically subscribed to a suite of individual journals through the services of serials subscription agents who would place orders with publishers. Direct contacts between librarians and publishers were infrequent. The ability to reshape a library's portfolio was straightforward, as individual titles could be added and canceled, and this allowed for changes in academic priorities, usage patterns, and budgets. Today, much content is licensed through subscriptions to so-called Big Deals, where a library will acquire a vast portion of, or all of, the titles issued by an individual publisher. The Big Deal is secured through negotiation between the library (or consortium) and the publisher, often for a contractually specified number of years, with annual price increases fixed for the duration of the license.

Big Deal licenses can be priced at millions of dollars for individual research universities, and librarians involved in negotiations need to prepare thoroughly. Most corporations develop playbooks to support negotiations (Menkel-Meadow and Dingwall, 2017), and it is suggested that librarians consider developing such playbooks to inform their priorities and negotiating points. The playbook is a document that gathers together a series of data and negotiating points for use by those working to update, revise, or renew a contract. A typical playbook might contain information about the publisher, including data about its business operations and finances, key items from press coverage and regulatory documents, and information about changes in its product portfolio. The playbook will also include data about the institution's use of the publisher's products (e.g., journals), including readership of content, articles published by members of the institution, and low-use content. Other relevant information might include details of the institution's faculty who serve on editorial boards or society committees and any other payment flows to the publisher (e.g., to license A&I databases or analytics platforms). Other notable relationships are R&D partnerships between the publisher and faculty, or workshops delivered by the publisher to graduate students. The intent is to gather as much information as possible about the publisher-institution relationship in order to assess the "value" of this relationship to the institution.

Developing a playbook can involve a wider team than solely those librarians who might meet a publisher's representatives for formal negotiation, including procurement and contracts specialists from the university's finance or legal departments and subject specialist librarians closely connected with those who create content for the publisher's journals. Business librarians are often good sources of company and market data and also might be invited to participate. The creation of this playbook could reasonably be led and coordinated by the library assessment team, representing particular expertise in data capture and analysis. Ideally, the playbook will not be created once and archived after use but rather form a living document updated regularly to reflect changes in the publishing marketplace and shifts in content usage and creation. Some components of the playbook, such as contract vocabulary and institutional procurement requirements, sit outside the scope of this chapter. However, aspects of the playbook relating to the librarians' understanding of the publisher and its business, data about historic usage of licensed content and the proportion that may now be freely available, shifts in the institution's academic priorities, and other institutional relations are addressed below.

Establishing Priorities

Depending on institutional needs, librarians might focus on achieving one or more of the following priorities: price reductions, maximizing the value of a given license, growing open-access opportunities, or securing access to a larger array of content. In some instances, librarians may need to negotiate cost savings either to accommodate overall budget reductions or to free up funds for alternative purchases. At other times, there may be a desire to maximize the perceived value of a package based on factors such as cost per use, the number of unused titles in a bundle, and impact on faculty productivity. Another desired outcome might be to incorporate open-access opportunities alongside continued readership access. Finally, a negotiation may seek to grow the volume of content available to an institution, for example, by gaining access to backfiles or by adding currently unsubscribed content with the lowest possible additional cost. Broadly, each of these represents a trade-off against the other: Few negotiations will maximize all of these!

In preparing for any negotiation, it is important to understand which of these priorities is of greatest importance, as this will influence the gathering and assessment of relevant data and other background information. Assigning these priorities will be influenced by current and forecast budget positions, an assessment of the comparative value of a given package, institutional postures toward open access, and user feedback on the adequacy of existing provisions of access to content. These priorities will form the first component of the playbook and will guide both the data to be gathered as well as the postures adopted by the negotiating team. The playbook will be populated with data considered necessary both to support the institution's particular priorities as well as to seek openings for additional gains.

Gathering Data

The Market Landscape and the Publisher's Business Environment

It is important to appreciate that just as the library team is developing its negotiating playbook, so too will the publisher's negotiating team. One of their key starting points will be an assessment of the desired value of the final contract, and this will be shaped by the company's particular financial situation as it prepares to negotiate. Many of the factors relevant to the publisher's position can be easily identified, and some time devoted to preparations can provide an informed perspective on the likely range of contract terms to be offered. Among others, publishers will have an eye to their global marketplace and the financial health of regional economies, as these can heavily impact sales and margins around the world, both in terms of overall ability to pay, and in the impact of exchange rate fluctuations (most publishers invoice in either U.S. dollars or Euros irrespective of the customer's location). Further, the financial health of different parts of their portfolios will be instrumental in determining the criticality of journal revenues. Some publishers operate primarily in the publishing world but may see their work segmented across research, professional, and trade publishing markets, each of which is likely to face different business cycles. The publisher might also be part of a conglomerate with business units operating across different industries. Finally, the publisher might seek funds to support growth, either through innovation and development, or mergers and acquisitions. All of these factors are likely to impact the "wiggle room" allowable even for the smallest license. Understanding a company's specific situation and plans, relative market pressures, and, where relevant, foreign currency movements can be tremendously useful. This can be achieved by monitoring the financial press and taking advice from colleagues in the university finance or investment offices. Another relevant factor to bear in mind is the time of year during which negotiations are taking place, and whether the lead negotiators are likely to be under an increased pressure to meet their individual sales targets. This sort of information is perhaps best assembled through tracking news about contract cancellations or major deals being recently concluded.

It can also be beneficial to regularly monitor the overall scholarly publishing landscape, tracking the flow of consolidations in the industry. The distribution of article publishing has become much more concentrated among a small number of large publishers over the past fifty years (Larivière et al., 2015), and there can be little doubt that this oligopoly has an impact on pricing and other contract terms. Technology investments made by publishers, for example, in digitizing backfiles, enriching content interoperability, and in growing platform functionality, all represent costs the publisher needs to recover and understanding the benefits of or lack of interest in these to a library's user base represent important points to be captured in the playbook.

The COVID-19 pandemic caused many university libraries to wrestle with extreme financial pressures, resulting in severe and potentially lasting budget reductions. These reductions will prioritize necessary and urgent negotiations to reduce spending. As far as possible, understanding overall budget pressures in the marketplace shapes how publishers are likely to respond. Some publishers may offer price stability for all customers; others may seek to pinpoint libraries with the ability to pay increased prices to offset losses from other customers. Entering negotiations with a sense of the overall position of other customers in the market is helpful and can often be gained from discussions among peers in consortia or organizations such as ARL and ALCTS.

Academic journal publishers typically operate as for-profit organizations (commercial publishers) or as core parts of learned and professional societies (society publishers). Commercial publishers (e.g., Wiley and Elsevier) may operate as publicly traded corporations, or as privately held entities (e.g., Springer Nature and SAGE). Companies listed on major stock exchanges are required to disclose information about business trends, revenues, risks, and pressures to allow investors to make informed decisions. A publicly traded publisher's website provides access to earnings presentations, financial results, and other statements on the company's market outlook. This information is valuable to librarians preparing for license negotiations and can readily be found in investor relations sections of publishers' websites or through company information databases licensed by many research libraries. The information availability will be determined by each countries' regulatory framework where the publisher is incorporated. In the United States, a Securities and Exchange Commission (SEC) filing includes a detailed assessment of business strategies, risks, and market analysis, which provide insights into company's goals and pathways to achieving them. Evaluating this information allows librarians to model the publisher's desired business outcomes and strengthen the library's position in negotiations. Wiley's First Quarter Fiscal 2021 Earning Review (United States Securities and Exchange Commission) and their 2020 Form 10-K Annual Report illustrate obtainable information for negotiations.

2021 First Quarter Fiscal

This report indicates favorable increases in publishing (up 5 percent), revenues (up 13 percent), and content usage (up 10 percent) over the previous year. In spite of challenges with university budgets, it forecasts continued double-digit access growth and nonlibrary revenue streams from universities.

In Wiley's report, the negotiating librarian may see this acknowledgment of 10 percent growth in use and difficulties with the library's budget as a helpful indication for negotiating acceptable pricing. They may also see presentations from Wiley on open-access solutions, as this is a growth opportunity for Wiley and may be an attempt to diversify revenue from library budgets or to work directly with researchers.

10-K Annual Report

This SEC-filed report provides business strategies, risks, market analysis, and the quality of Wiley's journal portfolio, based on Journal Citation Reports, which may be used by Wiley to negotiate higher annual prices. With this information, the library negotiator can focus on their institution's disciplinary priorities and a more nuanced negotiation based on how these disciplines performed in Wiley's portfolio.

Additionally, about half of Wiley's journal revenues come from professional society journals (e.g., American Chemical Society). These professional societies use faculty volunteers and are registered charities that receive an annual royalty from commercial publishers. Relevant information from society's IRS990 filings may become an important part of a negotiation playbook if they indicate publishing surpluses, which can amount to hundreds of millions of dollars yearly.

There is also a wealth of relevant information in the financial press and from market analyses issued by stockbrokers and other financial analysts. Outsell's *Industry Headlines* (https://www.outsellinc.com/headlines), Scholarly Kitchen (https://scholarlykitchen.sspnet.org/), and SPARC's *Big Deal Cancellation Tracking* (https://sparcopen.org/our-work/big-deal-cancellation-tracking/) are all good resources for information on industry news, about both commercial and society publishers.

Usage Data

Data can inform interactions with scholarly journal content. Researchers (faculty, research staff, and students) read, cite, and write. They may also serve as reviewers and editors. Additionally, librarians select, license, and point to journal content as part of their overall collections strategy. Each of these actions generates data that provides perspectives relevant to negotiations with publishers and can form the most important content in a negotiation playbook.

Across all of these sets of data, librarians are most actively engaged in generating data about journals use within their suite of licensed collections. These reports are produced monthly and include data on searches and downloads at the individual journal title level, allowing for easy calculations (e.g., cost per download) and for usage reporting between titles in a given portfolio to compare across different publishers. However, reports do not provide any granular data about users, such as their disciplinary affiliations. This detailed data can be gained by analyzing proxy server logs in conjunction with institutional records data. It should be noted that many institutions may not make use of proxy servers for on-campus users, preferring to use the faster and simpler IP address recognition. Understanding an institution's particular set-up informs the utility of proxy data. Also, the proxy logs format does not allow for straightforward analysis, and data cleanup is required. Resulting data may illustrate the distribution of readership across different journal titles and usage by an academic group, allowing for more informed campus engagement or, possibly, for internal recharge arrangements.

Publication Data

For research-intensive universities, the relationship between researchers and journal content extends to authorship. An important source of this data can be found from reference and citation data. Librarians can identify which journals are being cited by their institution's researchers' scholarship and track the citations to their publications. Both of these distinctive data-sets can influence negotiations. The librarian gains insights into the subscribed content's robustness and identifies cited materials not available in the library. This information may be useful for negotiations if the goal is to expand access to content that is in demand but currently unavailable. The three best-known sources of this data are Web of Science (https://clarivate.com/webofsciencegroup), Scopus (https://www.scopus.com/), and Dimensions (https://www.dimensions.ai/). APIs are generally available to download reference lists from publications authored by an institution's researchers. Data cleanup generates a ranked list of journal titles that can be matched against institutional subscriptions. Where needed, titles can be matched against publisher lists.

There are a few cautionary notes. In some fields, there has been a growing trend toward papers with vast numbers of coauthors, and it may not be feasible to associate a citation with any given library subscription. An author may retrieve an article from an open-access preprint server or institutional repository but cite the formal version of record. Thus, lack of an institutional subscription should not be assumed to highlight a deficiency.

Citation data of researchers' papers can be helpful in demonstrating the value of an institution's content to the publisher. For example, a series of highly cited articles increases a journal's impact factor and may be highly sought after by publishers. Stressing the importance of this material, and the close relations between librarians and researchers, can strengthen the librarians' negotiating position. This data is most useful when analyzed by the publisher.

All of this leads to more granular analyses. For example, librarians might wish to compare the relative significance of one publisher against another, either in terms of readership or volume of authored output. Such data also can be considered by discipline, using facets such as Field of Research codes or Web of Science subject categories provided in citation databases. Looking at the distribution of output in this way is informative to negotiations, allowing librarians to understand where their institution's particular needs and strengths may be located.

Publisher Data

In addition to tracking an institution's relationship with a publisher, as described previously, it can also be informative to understand some broad trajectories for a given publisher's portfolio (e.g., annual volume of journal titles and articles published, trends in journal impact factors, volume of articles published open access, and numbers of articles acknowledging particular research funders). This data, generated from citation indexes and verified against company reports and websites, can be useful to challenge (or accept) statements from publishers about the costs associated with increasing output, or the increase in "quality" of the content they publish.

Other Relationships

While the core relationship between an institution and a journal publisher can be viewed as broadly transactional—articles read, and articles cited and published—an institution may have many other interactions with a publisher. Understanding the extent of such engagement can be an important part of "selling" the importance of an institution to a publisher.

One such financial relationship is the flow of payments for services and content other than that covered by the license being negotiated. In some cases, this will relate to products also licensed by the library, for which data ought to readily be available in the electronic resource management or acquisitions systems. Typically, licenses for eBooks or conference series for indexing services and for printed materials might be seen. In some case other institution areas might license specific products (e.g., health and safe or lab-management tools). The range of research information managem/ services (e.g., Elsevier's Pure and Clarivate's InCites) might be licensed the research office. Another growing source of payments is individual o access APCs, often paid by individual authors from their research g Frequently, the best way to assemble such data is through a record in the finance or contracts office. The results can inform an approa references the depth of the financial relationship existing between organizations.

Another important consideration is the extent of researchers' ships with a publisher, including service as a reviewer, editor, or s role. Service on a society's board or committees might also be rel negotiating with a society publisher or a commercial publisher t services for a society. While this data can be difficult to gather, the depth of relationships and allows for more personalized negotiating.

Summary

The results of a major, multiyear journal license negotiatio implications for an institution. Journal content is valued providing point of need access is tremendously importa creasingly recognize the importance of open-access publi seamless pathways can lead to increased visibility and impact of their work, potentially yielding collaborations and future grant funding. Of course, the amount payable for a license has direct financial implications for the library, and the manner in which it can invest in competing priorities. For these reasons, the development of a playbook, with a strong focus on data to inform negotiations, is important.

This chapter set out some of the key components of a successful playbook, while recognizing that there are some areas that are inherently messy or difficult to quantify or interpret. For example, some society-owned journal titles change publishers every few years, a complicating data analysis. As open-access business models evolve, it has become common for payments and license arrangements to reflect corresponding authorship—that is, an article will be charged only to the institution employing the corresponding author. The corresponding author is not always readily identifiable in the data sources mentioned above.

Another key aspect of journal negotiations is the extent of the library's power. In practice, librarians have few options, except to walk away, resulting in undesirable situations like loss of content access. In such cases, close communication with the wider university community is an important task. Information generated during the preparation of the playbook can help inform conversations and negotiations.

Author Note

Monika M. Webster: https://orcid.org/0000-0003-0183-3904.
h G. Webster: https://orcid.org/0000-0003-4251-8660.

References

tion of Research Libraries (ARL) Annual Library Statistics. (2020, November 5). ARL Statistics. http://www.arlstatistics.org.

., Albee, B., and Romaine, S. (2020, April 14). *Costs outstrip library budgets periodicals price survey 2020.* Library Journal. https://www.libraryjournal. etailStory=Costs-Outstrip-Library-Budgets-Periodicals-Price-Survey-2020.

ns (n.d.). *Linked research data from idea to impact: Dimensions data and for discovery analytics.* Retrieved 1 September 2020, from https://www. ns.ai/

., Haustein, S., and Mongeon, P. (2015). The oligopoly of academic publishing in the digital era. *PLoS ONE, 10*(6), 1–15. https://doi.org/10.1371/journal. 502.

Menkel-Meadow, C., and Dingwall, R. (2017). Scripts: What to do when big bad companies won't negotiate. In C. Honeyman and A. K. Schneider (Eds.), *The negotiator's desk reference*. University of California Irvine. https://poseidon01.ssrn. com/delivery.php?ID=31610511110600709900312311009702609409705706901307903908508706610710500612207008207505403409810110201404210812309206611010609803702705308908402611707908106511712212305303301306908302102901507401907302401910702311.

Outsel (n.d.). *Outsell industry headlines*. Retrieved 5 September 2020, from https://www.outsellinc.com/headlines/.

SCOPUS. (n.d.). *Start exploring*. Retrieved 8 September 2020, from https://www.scopus.com.

Society for Scholarly Publishing. (n.d.). *The scholarly kitchen: What's hot and cooking in scholarly publishing*. Retrieved 4 September 2020, https://scholarlykitchen.sspnet.org/.

SPARC (n.d.). Big Deal Cancellation Tracking. SPARC. https://sparcopen.org/our-work/big-deal-cancellation-tracking/.

United States Securities and Exchange Commission. (2020, June 26). John Wiley and Sons, Inc. Form 10-K for Fiscal Year Ending 30 April 2020. Retrieved from https://wiley-ecomm-prod-content.s3.amazonaws.com/Investors+Filings/April_30_2020_10K.pdf.

Velterop, J. (2012). Reed Elsevier NV: Feedback from meeting with Jan Velterop. *FLASH NOTE*. Quoted in Dygert, Claire T. Honing your negotiation skills. NASIG Annual Conference 2012. Retrieved from https://dokumen.tips/education/honing-your-negotiation-skills.html

Wiley. (2020, September 3). First quarter fiscal 2021 earnings review. https://wiley-ecomm-prod-content.s3.amazonaws.com/Q121_Earnings_Presentation.pdf.

Additional Resources

Additional resources, not cited in this chapter, are recommended for further exploration.

Data Clean Up Tool Alteryx. (n.d.). *The Alteryx APA Platform Advantage*. Retrieved 10 September 2020, https://www.alteryx.com.

Data Clean Up Tool OpenRefine. (n.d.). https://openrefine.org/.

ezPAARSE (n.d.). https://ezpaarse-project.github.io/ezpaarse/.

Johnson, R., Watkinson, A., and Mabe, M. (2018). *The STM report: An overview of scientific and scholarly publishing* (fifth edition). International Association of Scientific, Technical and Medical Publishers, The Netherlands. https://www.stm-assoc.org/2018_10_04_STM_Report_2018.pdf.

OCLC Ezproxy (n.d.). https://www.oclc.org/en/ezproxy.html.

Project Counter (n.d.). https://www.projectcounter.org.

Title Comparison CrossRef. (n.d.). https://www.crossref.org/.

CHAPTER NINE

Space Assessments

Holt Zaugg

Faculty and students are often heard to say, "Oh, I never go to the library. I just look up what I need online!" They lack the understanding that both online and the brick-and-mortar building are library spaces. This chapter discusses assessments involving both spaces.

Online Spaces

Online library access is an outward-facing service (see chapter 2), but it can also be assessed as an online space that allows patrons to use the library without being physically present. The library's website is the conduit to this virtual space that enables library patrons to obtain resources and access services virtually, which is increasingly important as more and more patrons access library resources and services via the website portal. When assessing online library spaces, it is helpful to have a virtual floor plan of where patrons can go and how they can get there. This virtual floor plan allows you to examine online spaces in a way that is understandable to those building, populating, and using the space.

Physical Spaces

Assessments of physical spaces range from incredibly simple to complex because of multiple library locations, offsite storage, and renovations that meld older buildings to newer structures. Assessment of physical spaces also deals with everything inside the library's walls and how the study, storage, and instruction spaces are designed and used. For example, is furniture stationary? Or can patrons move and adjust it to meet their needs? Is a space intended for a single person to quietly focus on learning tasks? Or is it built for two or more people to collaborate? Does the alignment of stacks facilitate clear and safe lines of sight? Similar to online spaces, it is good to begin with a floor plan to understand the space you are about to evaluate.

The four aspects of assessment from chapter 1 are discussed in terms of their fit to online and physical space assessments. Where possible, assessments should consider how the library spaces may influence each other, especially when a patron is visiting an online library space while sitting in a physical library space.

Design

Assessments of library spaces are facilitated by a map showing online or physical spaces and information regarding who uses the spaces so that the best approach to collecting data can be determined (Kaufman et al., 2018; Prentice and Argyropoulos, 2018). A good first step is to conduct a baseline inventory describing the spaces and what is in them. It is also helpful to develop or use academic library personas to understand library-use behaviors associated with groups of patrons (Zaugg and Rackham, 2016; Zaugg, 2017; Zaugg and Ziegenfuss, 2018). Combining these two steps allows evaluators to understand what is in the library space and how it is used. A baseline inventory and personas help library personnel see spaces with users' eyes as they examine how the spaces are used.

With this increased understanding, evaluators choose from a variety of assessment methods to collect data (Corrall, 2017). When data collection involves students, student researchers should be trained and used to collect data where possible, as they are similar to patrons using the space and are better able to elicit honest, open responses from student participants (Washburn and Bibb, 2011).

Data Collection

This section discusses six assessment tools that are uniquely suited to examining online and physical spaces: logs, surveys, ethnographies or usability tests, interviews or focus groups, observations, and photo studies. There are other options for data collection. The method and personnel used to collect the data should suit the space being assessed (Trembach et al., 2019).

Logs

Murphy (2019), at Ohio State University, developed a process to extract and clean EZ Proxy logs on a daily basis. The log data was married with demographic data and displayed in Tableau to create a one-and-a-half-million-row dataset. Those accessing this data could disaggregate it by dates, status, or department/major to inform decision-making.

At BYU, the university's IT department links these two datasets to protect the patron's privacy but allows disaggregation of use patterns (see figure 9.1). In this example, library EZ Proxy requests are tracked and disaggregated by the web link for the request, continent, country, college campus or school, and year. Additional links between the library and university demographic data can show use patterns and trends of specific groups (e.g., students in online courses or study abroad or internship programs). Knowing use patterns helps the library assist those in these groups find and use the resources or

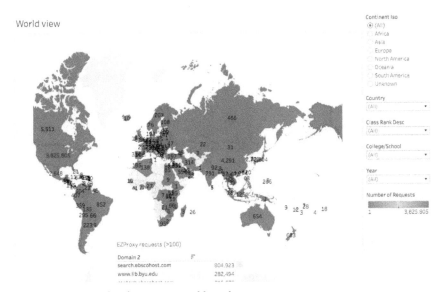

Figure 9.1.   Example of EZ Proxy Dashboard. Zaugg

services housed in this online space. The data also establishes baseline data so that changes can be compared to determine if the change was helpful or not. Additional log information may track library entrances and exits, check outs of library materials, reservations of study or instruction rooms, public computer use, patron movement, and occupancy by library space, to name a few.

Surveys

Torres and Paul (2019), at the Dibner Library serving the NYU-Tandon School of Engineering, used Qualtrics as a record-keeping tool where library employees set the Qualtrics survey up so that count data for defined library spaces could be easily counted and entered. Using the survey tool in this way helped to prevent errors that may occur when transcribing from paper to online storage.

Pop-up, paper, and poster invitations may be used to invite students to participate in a survey. For example, when students logged on to a public-access computer, a pop-up invitation asked them to participate in a survey about why they use the library's public-access computers with the options of "yes," "not now," and "no." Depending on the response, students were directed to the online survey, returned to the pop-up queue, or excluded from other requests. In another instance, paper surveys were placed on old independent-study desks, asking students how they used the study space and what would improve the desk. Once completed, the survey was turned in at a nearby reference desk in exchange for a mini chocolate bar. This method worked surprisingly well for getting surveys turned in, but the candy disap-peared at a rate faster than surveys were turned in—the cost of using hungry reference desk student employees. Finally, to evaluate the furniture in a newly refurbished study space and how students used it, a poster with a QR code and URL link invited participation and incentivized survey comple-tion with a draw for a cash award (Zaugg and Belliston, 2020). Surprisingly, the cost of mini chocolate bars and the cost of the incentive were about the same!

Ethnographies or Usability Tests

A scripted ethnography examined pathways students used to find people, resources, or locations in twelve scenarios, each beginning at the entrance to the library (Zaugg et al., 2016). High school senior students, freshman, and senior college students completed the tasks to provide a range of patron experiences. Two or three student researchers took field notes and video recorded each participant as they moved along their pathway to complete each task. The participant talked about decisions along their pathway and completed a short interview about their experience. This scripted ethnography provided insights on what students do and do not use to navigate their way through the library.

The usability test is the online equivalent of an ethnography. Students are asked to find a virtual location starting at the library's website. Data is collected via video recordings, field notes, and screen-capture technology, while the students talk their way through the task. Usability tasks may be completed individually or in small groups while the evaluator asks them questions or just observes what they are doing.

Interviews or Focus Groups

Interviews and focus groups may be used with another assessment tool or independently in quick stop-and-answer questions in a public setting, or in a more private location with a longer set of questions. Both explore the students' experience with the library space using a mix of questions, including specific questions about a particular feature and open-ended questions for broader, more in-depth responses. For virtual spaces, students may be shown the space and asked questions regarding its aesthetics, navigability, or some other feature. Just after the release of a new website design, focus groups were shown the website and asked about its look, feel, and ease of use (Rennick, 2019). This assessment provided improvement information and baseline data for a follow-up assessment several years later.

Public in-person interviews should occur in a way that is not disruptive to other students or intrusive on participants' time. In one assessment, we placed two redesigned independent-study desks near the main entrance to the library, but off to the side. As students passed by, we asked them to look at and try the prototype desks and let us know what they did and did not like. The assessment helped us quickly refine the desks to best meet student needs.

Observations

Observations may also be used independently or as part of another assessment tool. They may be as simple as walking through a space and counting the number of students using different types of furniture or as complex as watching interactions in group study rooms over a period of time. The intent is to see how students interact with the space. As mentioned earlier, students could be given specific tasks, or evaluators may just watch what happens. Video recordings may also capture observations, but it is advisable to post that the space is being video recorded for improvement purposes. Observational data and input from students are particularly important when designing and assessing the efficacy of unique spaces specifically designed for student groups, such as young families (Graff et al., 2019; Moore et al., 2020).

Photo Studies

The Stark Campus Library of Kent State University used a picture assessment in conjunction with two types of observations—one that counted the number of students using a given space, and another observation that recorded the setting, activities, and significant occurrences focused on group versus individual or quiet versus noise settings (Bauer, 2020). The photo study asked participants to take photographs of different spaces using thirteen prompts. There was also a thirty-minute follow-up interview. The data was analyzed using thematic qualitative techniques to provide a deeper and stronger picture of how students use the library and what additional changes would benefit their learning activities.

Data Analysis

Data analysis follows prescribed quantitative and qualitative methods. Prior to data collection, it is essential to know how the data will be analyzed. For videos and log data, start and end times may be used to examine time-of-day, day-of-week, and length-of-use data. If a change is made and statistical analysis is helpful, this data can be used to indicate significant differences. Qualitative data may use grids and themes to analyze observations of interactions. Maps of physical and online spaces may also be used to provide samples of pathways along with success and fail points.

Dissemination

Once analysis is completed, dissemination should include reports to specified stakeholders and may include dissemination at conferences and in journals. Some data may be displayed in interactive dashboards, as discussed earlier, where stakeholders may examine data and periodically return to see trends and patterns. It may also be helpful to have sample videos to illustrate key points of use or methods for data collection.

Value and Decision-Making

Assessments of online and physical spaces provide a strong value description for the library, as they are the face of the library. The look, feel, and utility of these spaces defines the library, as it invites or dissuades students from using it. When library space assessments are combined or integrated with campus-wide plans, the library gains a seat at the table in planning, and its spaces are developed to augment changes to learning spaces on campus (Ozburn et al., 2020). Seeking student and library-employee input becomes critical to the success of changes within the library.

Summary

Space assessments are important because they examine virtual and physical spaces, which are the public face of the library and help to determine the success of all that the library does. Using a variety of data collection methods provides multiple perspectives of a space so that it is inviting and easy to use. The temptation is to think of space as a thing instead of an environment that encourages or dissuades people to be there. Careful collection and analysis of data helps inform what the needs and desires of those people are instead of just assuming that you know what is best.

References

Bauer, M. (2020). Commuter students and the academic library: A mixed-methods study of space. *Journal of Library Administration*, 60(2), 146–54.

Corrall, S. (2017). Library space assessment methods: Perspectives of new information professionals. *Information and Learning Science*, 119(1/2), 39–63.

Graff, T., Ridge, R. D., and Zaugg, H. (2019). A space for every student: Assessing the utility of a family friendly study room in a university library. *Journal of Library Administration*, 59(6), 629–55.

Kaufman, J., Dosch, B., and Clement, K. A. (2018). No failure, just feedback: A reflection on experiential space assessment in an academic library. *Serials Review*, 44(3), 221–27.

Moore, A. C., Croxton, R., and Sprague, L. (2020). Breaking down barriers for student parents and caregivers with family-friendly library spaces. *Journal of Library Administration*, 60(3), 215–34.

Murphy, S. A. (2019). A non-programmers guide to enhancing and making sense of EZ Proxy logs. *Performance Measurement and Metrics*, 20(3), 186–95.

Ozburn, L., Kirk, J., and Eastman, T. (2020). Creating collaborative library spaces through partnerships with campus organizations. *Journal of Library Administration*, 60(6), 600–12.

Prentice, K. A., and Argyropoulos, E. K. (2018). Library space: Assessment and planning through a space utilization study. *Medical Reference Services Quarterly*, 37(2), 132–41.

Rennick, B. (2019). Library services navigation: Improving the online user experience. *Information Technology and Libraries*, *38*(1), 14–26.

Torres, A., and Paul, G. (2019). Reaching maximum occupancy: What the numbers tell us about space and ways to improve services. *Journal of Access Services*, *16*(2–3), 78–93.

Trembach, S., Blodgett, J., Epperson, A., and Floersch, N. (2019). The whys and hows of academic library space assessment: A case study. *Library Management*, *41*(1), 28–38.

Washburn, A., and Bibb, S. C. (2011). Students studying students: An assessment of using undergraduate student researchers in an ethnographic study of library use. *Library and Information Research*, *35*(109), 55–66.

Zaugg, H. (2017). Using persona descriptions to inform library space design. In S. Schmehl Hines and K. Moore Crowe (Eds.), *Advances in library administration and organization: Vol. 36. The future of library space* (pp. 335–58). Emerald.

Zaugg, H., and Belliston, C. J. (2020). Assessing old and new individual study desks. *Performance Measurement and Metrics*, *21*(2), 93–106.

Zaugg, H., Child, C., Bennett, D., Brown, J., Alcaraz, M., Allred, A., Andrus, N., Babcock, D., Barriga, M., Brown, M., Bulloch, L., Corbett, T., Curtin, M., Giossi, V., Hawkins, S., Hernandez, S., Jacobs, K., Jones, J., Kessler, D. . . . and Zandamela, T. (2016). Comparing library wayfinding among novices and experts. *Performance Measurement and Metrics*, *17*(1), 70–82.

Zaugg, H., and Rackham, S. (2016). Identification and development of patron personas for an academic library. *Performance Measurement and Metrics*, *17*(2), 124–33.

Zaugg, H., and Ziegenfuss, D. (2018). Comparison of personas between two academic libraries. *Performance Measurement and Metrics*, *19*(3), 142–52.

~

CHAPTER TEN

Creating Space with Our Community in Mind

A Library Building Assessment Toolkit

Barbara Ghilardi, Fairfield University

The DiMenna-Nyselius Library creates a welcoming and friendly atmosphere that encompasses services, collections, and the physical space. A toolkit of building-usage studies was developed and administered between fall 2016 and fall 2019. This chapter discusses the tools' methodologies and what was learned, along with challenges and future considerations. As more campuses reimagine what student gathering and study spaces look like, advocating for additional student space in the library can be challenging. This chapter demonstrates how academic libraries with minimal resources can build a customizable, effective building assessment toolkit that could be used as needed to generate meaningful data.

Background

Fairfield University is a residential campus with a full time equivalent (FTE) of 5,500 undergraduate and graduate students. The DiMenna-Nyselius Library was constructed in 1968, expanded in 2001, and again in summer 2019. The main floor was renovated to include five other campus departments that support student learning. This renovated space is now called the Academic

Commons. The building-usage studies presented in this chapter evaluate the physical library space and library services.

The library began creating a culture of assessment in spring 2015 with the formation of an assessment committee. This committee created library-learning goals and student-learning outcomes, focused on assessing library space. Previously, visits were tracked using a gate counter, and no other building assessment projects were developed. Given the high usage of the space, it would be easy to assume all physical spaces worked well for our users. However, without concrete data, library employees were not sure if spaces were actually meeting users' needs, or if the library was just a convenient place.

Employees wondered why students studied in the library instead of other places on campus. After conducting an extensive review of research that measured building usage, the committee was inspired by the work done at Wright State University Libraries using a tool called SUMA (Casden and Davidson, 2013), which tracks the number of people in spaces throughout the library. Additionally, a questionnaire was placed at different seats around the library (Shannon et al., 2015). The committee determined a flexible toolkit of building assessment projects should be created. A four-part mixed methods study was conducted over the course of the fall 2016 and spring 2017 semesters, specifically during the university's final exam period (Ferree and Kremer, 2017). Data provided useful information to the staff for small, immediate changes to the building and services but was also useful when the university expressed interest in creating an Academic Commons within the library. The assessment committee provided the reports of all studies conducted to both library and university administration.

In the summer of 2019, the library's main floor was renovated to include spaces for five academic departments. A computer lab located in the lobby of the library was renovated by the College of Arts and Sciences into the Fredrickson Family Innovation Lab, and new furniture was purchased. The library's café was expanded, creating space for desktop computers and more seating. Staff offices were added to the library's upper level, changing some of the seating arrangements there. These changes provided an opportune time to utilize the toolkit again in order to discern whether renovated spaces changed library users' general feelings about studying in the library or the way they used the building.

Toolkit

Below is a summary of each building-usage study conducted, including methodology, what was learned, and limitations and future considerations.

SUMA Building-Usage Study (Fall 2016 and Fall 2019)

Methodology

SUMA is an open-source tablet-based tool developed at NC State University Libraries. The purpose of the tool is to "collect and analyze observational data about the usage of physical spaces and services" (Casden et al., 2020). Student workers and librarians used the tool to do a headcount of everyone in library spaces. The goal in December 2016 was to see how busy the library was during finals. Library use was tracked in specific areas three times during the day (11:00 a.m., 4:00 p.m., and 9:00 p.m.) over an eleven-day period. Each library area was named and programmed into SUMA, ensuring consistency. SUMA summed all counts and uploaded them into Microsoft Excel. The study was repeated in 2019 to see how busy the library was in comparison to three other buildings on campus with student study spaces—Egan School of Nursing, Dolan School of Business, and Barone Campus Center. Student and library employees counted the number of people in each place at 2:00 p.m., 5:00 p.m., and 9:00 p.m.

What Was Learned

The library tends to be busiest during the late afternoon and early evening. In 2016, the building was 60 percent busier on average at 4:00 p.m. than it was at 11:00 a.m. and 9:00 p.m. Similarly, during the 2019 study, occupancy was highest at 5:00 p.m. This trend also held in the Barone Campus Center and Dolan School of Business. In the Egan School of Nursing, the average number of students studying increased by 56 percent at 9:00 p.m., suggesting that students may be in classes or at work during the day. In 2016, the study was during finals, so the library was at its busiest, and most spaces were at their maximum capacity. In 2019, all four buildings did not go over 30 percent capacity, suggesting that in the middle of the semester students may study in their dorm or their workloads may not have yet increased.

Limitations and Future Considerations

More efforts were made to put out extra furniture from storage during finals exams in spring 2017, and more events were created to engage the students in the library. The 2019 study demonstrated that the building was the busiest building on campus on that day during those times. However, it does not show this is the case over the course of a week or a longer time period. A semester-long space-usage study using SUMA would be useful to see trends to determine if expanding library space (e.g., study rooms) is needed.

The amount of student and library-staff time must also be considered, which could limit this study as well as the number of available iPads.

Photographic Ethnography Study (Fall 2016 and Fall 2019)

Methodology

This study used digital photography to document how students used different library spaces. Photos of the same space on all three floors were taken by one person at 11:00 a.m., 4:00 p.m., and 9:00 p.m. In 2016, this study was conducted during two reading days prior to final exams. In fall 2019, two days in November were chosen to see how the renovation changed the way the space was used.

What Was Learned

Clear patterns in the furniture use were seen. In both instances of the study, students liked to spread out their items on long tables (see figure 10.1). Each table seats six people, but only two to four students could comfortably sit at them. Carrels were popular, even on the main floor where there is more foot traffic, indicating that privacy does not mean isolation. Students want to be seen or see others even when they are studying alone. Most students chose seats where an outlet was available and, if necessary, extension cords were used. Most of the large tables and carrels have power, but some carrels on the second floor did not have power, and in 2019, they were not often used. Once power strips and wall outlets were added, they became popular. In 2019, the furniture in the library café was very cluttered and close together, deterring people from sitting there. A change to the layout of the room provided more space between tables, increasing students' use. Both studies observed that students gravitated toward the lower level of the building when they wanted quiet, particularly later in the day. The upper level was busiest earlier in the day when students wanted to sit near windows for natural light. Natural light was mentioned as a student preference in other surveys.

Limitations and Future Considerations

In 2016, this study was done during reading days, arguably some of the busiest days during the year, when the same students were in the same space for long periods of time. In 2019, the building was much quieter, as data was collected during the semester. Future studies should collect data at the same time of the semester and the same time of day to facilitate comparisons.

Figure 10.1. Student Working at a Table on Upper Level, Photographic Ethnography Study, December 2016, 11 a.m. Ghilardi

Student Library Advisory Board (SLAB) Focus Group (Fall 2017)

Methodology

Fifteen undergraduate and graduate student representatives from multiple disciplines and class years serve on SLAB. Groups of two or three students were prompted to draw their ideal library workspace on large sheets of paper. A discussion followed this exercise where librarians asked students questions to clarify their drawings (see figure 10.2).

What Was Learned

Students expressed a desire for multiple types of workspaces, including spaces for quiet, focused work and spaces for group work or conversation. Noise was a concern for all groups. They recommended clear signage to indicate which areas or floors are for quiet study and where noise is allowed. Evaluators noted a desire for quiet space did not necessarily mean isolated space, something that came up in other studies. Students expressed the need for more café food options, so they could take a break to eat but not necessarily leave the building. They wanted the library's atmosphere to be cozy and welcoming.

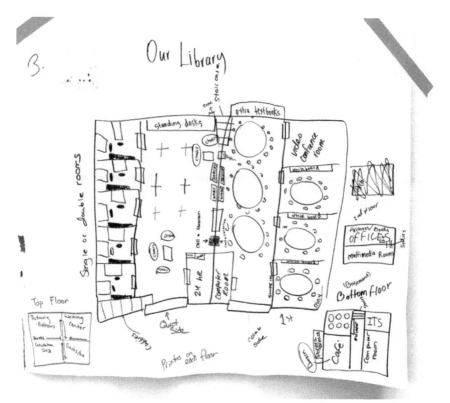

Figure 10.2. Student Library Advisory Board Focus Group Drawing of Ideal Library Space, October 2017. Ghilardi

Limitations and Future Considerations

The SLAB students were valuable in providing feedback on the building and services. Their candid remarks were appreciated. Some of their ideal drawings suggested ideas that could never be implemented, such as building another floor and adding a Panera to the library. However, more comfortable furniture, tables in the café, and more food options were possible and offered. In 2019, computers were put in the café per student suggestions. While all students' voices are important, this feedback is from a select group who use the library most often, which might have colored their responses.

Why Did You Choose This Seat? (Spring 2017 and Fall 2019)

Methodology

In order to capture authentic feelings of why a student might choose a certain seat in the library, a survey, with multiple-choice and open-ended questions, was developed and placed at each seat in the library at the beginning of each day with completed surveys collected and replaced four times throughout the day. Completed surveys were coded to the location, furniture type, time of day, and day it was completed.

This study was first conducted in April 2017 for ten days during finals and repeated in November 2019 for five days. In 2017, students were asked why they chose the seat and location with clarifying comments, and what they would change about the library. In 2019, the open-ended section used one question to ask students to describe their ideal study space in the library. Coding was consistent for both 2017 and 2019 (see figure 10.3), but students

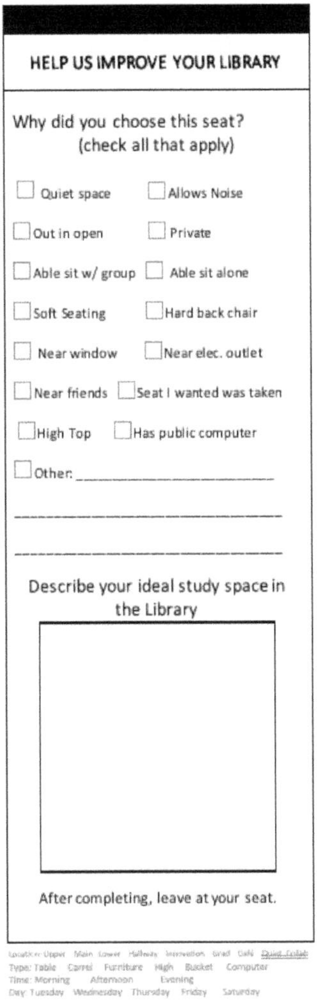

HELP US IMPROVE YOUR LIBRARY

Why did you choose this seat?
(check all that apply)

☐ Quiet space   ☐ Allows Noise

☐ Out in open   ☐ Private

☐ Able sit w/ group ☐ Able sit alone

☐ Soft Seating   ☐ Hard back chair

☐ Near window   ☐ Near elec. outlet

☐ Near friends ☐ Seat I wanted was taken

☐ High Top   ☐ Has public computer

☐ Other: _____
_____
_____

Figure 10.3. Why Did You Choose This Seat? Survey, November 2019. Ghilardi

Describe your ideal study space in
the Library

After completing, leave at your seat.

Location: Upper Main Lower Hallway Innovation Grad Café Quiet Zones
Type: Table Carrel Furniture High Basket Computer
Time: Morning Afternoon Evening
Day: Tuesday Wednesday Thursday Friday Saturday

taking the survey were asked to indicate the day and time in 2019, and library employees who collected the surveys coded the location and furniture type. Survey responses were manually entered into an Excel spreadsheet for analysis. There were 338 responses in 2017 and 368 responses in 2019.

What Was Learned

"Quiet" followed by "access to outlets" were the most popular reasons someone chose their seat in both 2017 and 2019. In 2019, a few students commented that the noise level on the main floor had increased since the renovation, possibly because all of the Academic Commons partners' offices on this floor. Furniture also played a role in seat choice. In spring 2017, 81 percent of students who filled out the survey sat at a table. In fall 2019, this rate dropped to 58 percent, but tables were still the most popular type of furniture. Carrels were the next popular type of furniture, selected by students at a rate of 31 percent in 2017 and 20 percent in 2019. Students commented that they liked carrels, as they helped stave off distractions. Armchairs were an option in both studies, but only made up only 5 percent of responses, suggesting that armchairs are not as popular. When students mention wanting "cozy" or "comfortable" seating, they are referring to the hardback chairs that have a cushion on the seat. When some chairs were put in storage, only chairs without cushions were taken away. This feedback also influences future furniture purchases; seats without cushions will be replaced with cushioned chairs.

Limitations and Future Considerations

This study took considerable time from student workers and librarians. Tasks included putting out and collecting surveys and entering data into Excel, which may have resulted in additional errors. There were also issues training students in collecting and coding surveys, which meant some surveys did not have the location and furniture type. In the future, everyone will be properly trained.

VIP Study Room Survey (Fall 2019)

Methodology

An online survey was created using LibWizard and sent over the University's Life@Fairfield portal to all students inviting them to enter for a chance to win a VIP study room (a study room reserved exclusively for them) in the library during finals. To enter, students were asked (1) what they liked best about the new Academic Commons space, (2) what services they use in the building, and (3) what they want to see changed (see appendix). The survey was open for three days, and 492 people responded. All data was exported from LibWizard to Excel for coding.

What Was Learned

When students were asked what they liked best about the library building, 27 percent said they liked the atmosphere and appearance, using words like "comfy," "cozy," "comfortable," "aesthetic," and "atmosphere" to describe the look and feel of the library. This is a reminder that what the library looks like matters and is the reason some may, or may not, study in the building.

Group study rooms were popular, with 29 percent of students naming them as a service they used. Group study rooms added as part of the main level renovation were heavily used. When asked what they would like to see changed, 20 percent of students indicated more seating. Several comments said that there were not enough restrooms or that existing ones did not have enough stalls. In response, both bathrooms on the upper level were changed into unisex bathrooms. Almost half (49 percent) of students wanted some place quiet to study, but others wanted a section where more noise is allowed, specifically for groups. In response, more signage was added to denoted quiet areas, and students are provided earplugs at the library services and information desk. Nevertheless, the building design includes an atrium where noise carries. The second most popular answer for what students wanted changed was none (19 percent).

Limitations and Future Considerations

While all students were invited to take the survey, there were few responses from students who do not regularly use the library. Future surveys could potentially be administered through our Office of Institutional Research to reach these students to provide a window into why students may not find the library space as welcoming or conducive to their studies.

Summary

The building-usage studies over the last few years provided insights into how the community uses library space and what it expects. There are plans to continue to use a combination of these studies every few semesters. It is most important that these studies are not done in a vacuum and that the data is acted on in the short-term and long-term.

Ultimately, the studies show that students need a variety of furniture and spaces. Librarians should be cognizant of this when purchasing furniture and reimagining space. Capturing students' voices is important, and their comments have proven to be most beneficial in giving insight into the library spaces and services. Collected data will be used in the future to inform building and service changes. There is great value in assessing building space, especially when the library has a central location on most campuses and is heavily used by students. This flexible toolkit is easily customizable and could be used at any academic library.

References

Casden, J., and Davidson, B. (2013, April 11). *The SUMA project: Integrating observational data assessment into space and service design* (conference session). Association of College and Research Libraries 2013 Cyber Zed Shed track, Indianapolis, IN. https://speakerdeck.com/bretdavidson/the-suma-project-integrating-observational-data-assessment-into-space-and-service-design.

Casden, J., Rucker, R., Aeschleman, L., Davidson, B., and Beswick, K. (2020). *SUMA: A tablet-based toolkit for collecting, managing, and analyzing data about the usage of physical spaces.* NC State University Libraries. https://www.lib.ncsu.edu/projects/suma.

Ferree, C., and Kremer, J. (2017, October 13). *Saving space: Collecting building-usage data to advocate for student space in the library* (conference session). Dartmouth Library October Conference. https://digitalcommons.dartmouth.edu/cgi/viewcontent.cgi?article=1006&context=octconf.

Shannon, M., Polanka, S., and Sydelko, B. S. (2015, July 15). *Driving the bus: Building use study and space assessment at Wright State University Libraries* (conference session). OHIO Dive Into Data. https://corescholar.libraries.wright.edu/ul_pub/171.

Additional Resources

Assessments that are not cited in this chapter but were used for the toolbox development.

DiMenna-Nyselius Library. (2016a, December). Building headcounts: An observational usage study. https://www.fairfield.edu/library/about/assessment/reports/SUMA_Report_DEC2016_REV.pdf.

DiMenna-Nyselius Library. (2016b, December). Photographic ethnography approach: An observational usage study. https://www.fairfield.edu/library/about/assessment/reports/Photos_Ethnography_dec2016_report_FINAL.pdf.

DiMenna-Nyselius Library. (2017a). Draw your ideal library space: Student library advisory board focus group. https://libraryapps.fairfield.edu/cdn/assessment/SLAB_library_space_Report_OCT172017_2.pdf.

DiMenna-Nyselius Library. (2017b, April/May). Student seating choice survey. https://www.fairfield.edu/media/fairfielduniversitywebsite/images/library/docu ments/Student%20Seat%20Choice%20Survey%20Report%20FINAL.pdf.
DiMenna-Nyselius Library. (2019a). Photographic ethnography approach: An observational usage study. https://www.fairfield.edu/library/about/assessment/reports/ Building-Utilization-Photo-Study-2019-Report.pdf.
DiMenna-Nyselius Library. (2019b). SUMA building usage study. https://www.fair field.edu/library/about/assessment/reports/SUMA-report.pdf.
DiMenna-Nyselius Library. (2019c). VIP study room academic commons survey. https://www.fairfield.edu/library/about/assessment/reports/VIP-Study-Room-AC -Survey-Dec-2019-REPORT.pdf.
DiMenna-Nyselius Library. (2019d). Why did you choose this seat? https://www .fairfield.edu/library/about/assessment/reports/wdycts_report.pdf.

Appendix: VIP Study Room Survey, December 2019

Select the date(s) that you would like to use the VIP study room. (required)
Tuesday, Dec. 10
Wednesday, Dec. 11
Over the summer the Library went through a renovation.
What do you like best about the building? (required)
Which services do you use in the building? (required)
What would you like to see changed? (required)
To enter the raffle for the VIP Study Room please enter your FAIRFIELD email address.

~

CHAPTER ELEVEN

Space Assessment Pre-Op

Operational Considerations when Space Planning for Libraries

Joelle Pitts, Carnegie Mellon University Libraries

Until the latter half of the twentieth century, library spaces remained relatively unchanged, as they served their communities by purchasing, housing, and organizing the materials that support scholarship. The rise of research libraries and the information literacy movement in the latter half of the twentieth century fueled a gradual shift away from repository and preservation models toward library materials accessibility and increased use (Weiner, 2005). The impact of the digital era on academic libraries resulted in adapting at a greater rate than ever before to meet the changing needs of campus communities. The design of library environments included consideration of newly opened space resulting from these shifts, as academic libraries consider their changing roles as facilitators of self-directed learning and the creation of new knowledge (Nitecki, 2011).

A compounding effect is that many libraries have postponed large renovation and remodeling projects over the last decade, with a few notable exceptions. Smaller, more typical renovation projects are usually a byproduct of community needs for more technology-enabled collaborative spaces, large-scale weeding of outdated print collections, or the introduction of shared space with other organizations. Many libraries may build on the print-to-digital transformation as a means to build relevancy (Palfrey, 2015). These attempts to transition physical spaces to meet the needs of campus communities will likely be unique to each campus depending on how new space design supports libraries and their services (Nitecki, 2011).

The most successful attempts are prefaced by a space and needs assessment. Before any targeted space assessments can proceed, library administrators and project staff must have a baseline understanding of the building and operational elements underlying any space change. This chapter focuses on a structural-level assessment of library spaces and facilities, a space assessment "pre-op" that offers a foundation from which any space project can begin. The following categories delve into considerations and best practices, augmented by recent examples, and followed by a comprehensive checklist.

Budget

Nothing thwarts a renovation faster than a poorly developed budget. With college and university libraries digging deeper than ever to fund soaring subscription costs, allocating funding for capital improvement projects can be incredibly challenging, especially as design and construction costs can quickly reach into the millions. In many cases, money needs to be spent on a design study or facilities bid just to understand how much the project will cost. Large project planning typically occurs over several months and years, so accounting for inflation of project costs is also wise, as is timing of project components. Summer is a peak construction window for higher education space projects, and the costs of crews and materials rise according to the market.

Pre-Op Budget Examples

The ALA Library Construction and Renovation site (2014) and Garcia (2019) provide some examples of library development projects and their costs.

- A $774,000 roofing project at Kansas State University's (K-State) Hale Library ballooned into a nearly $100-million restoration project after an accidental fire (Garcia, 2019).
- Dixie State University's learning commons is a campus information hub by sharing space with the English Department, a writing center, career services, and the IT Department, allowing easy access to services in one building. ($41 million)
- Saint Joseph's University updated its library to bring it fully into the digital age with a 35,000-square-foot learning commons, offering the

latest technologies, including a video-capable presentation practice room; an audiovisual multimedia lab; and a digital media zone with dual-monitor computers, comprehensive research content, and the latest software. ($16 million)

- Anne Arundel Community College renovated and expanded its library focusing on technology by adding twenty tech-rich collaboration rooms and two information literacy labs tied together by a large commons area featuring quick-access computer kiosks. ($16.8 million)

Nationwide, colleges and universities spent $12 billion per year from 2014 through 2016 on new construction and renovations (Marcus, 2017). Administrators need to understand what the project might cost, assume it will cost at least 5 percent to 10 percent more than planned (the going rate of contingency coverage for many lenders), and start allocating or searching for funds immediately. Some libraries manage to save for several years to afford these types of projects. Others convince university administration or donors with deep pockets that the cause is worthy. Some carve the funds out of their collection budgets, one canceled subscription at a time. Some university libraries share funding and spaces with other offices and service providers on campus who need to be engaged and in agreement on any space project. The following section explores these dynamics.

Project Team

Planning for new spaces can be exciting, and it may be tempting to kick off space projects by forming a library project team to work on the design specifications. As with any complex operation, however, the right people must be in the room and have a good understanding of the underlying conditions and workflows that help or hinder progress. The first project team members should not be library employees—library perspectives come in later. The initial team should come from campus facilities, financial, regulatory, and safety offices. In some cases, a representative from a development office or even the office of general counsel is necessary. Human health and safety offices can help preparations for worker accommodations required during construction. The local fire marshal can advise on the code review process before the project is in violation.

One fairly common example of the need to bring a facilities representative into early conversations is the possibility of the presence of lead paint, asbestos, or other hazardous materials. Buildings constructed from the 1930s until the 1970s likely contain some asbestos, which is harmful to human skin and respiratory systems when inhaled (United States Environmental Protection Agency, n.d.). Asbestos abatement is federally regulated and expensive. Campus facilities representatives might have maps or other information that can help determine where and how much asbestos is located in the affected areas.

This list of offices and individuals to contact depends on campus procedures and protocols. Facilities, campus design, and human health and safety are the most obvious and important, but it may also include external stakeholders such as architects, designers, contractors, insurance agents, and donors. Take the time to reach out to these various entities, write down the names of those spoken with, and take notes on any documentation offered. Hire a temporary project manager, or reassign someone, if this level of focus isn't possible given current workloads. Ideally, a project lead will be very familiar with library spaces and already have established operational connections across campus.

Project Team Examples

At Carnegie Mellon University (CMU), most buildings, including the library, were constructed with asbestos. Most building projects include asbestos abatement, a process exacerbated by the type of materials housed in the space. The abatement and modest ceiling and flooring refresh in the CMU Fine and Rare Books Room required involvement from seven library staff and faculty and representatives from four different offices on campus and cost over $240,000.

For several months after the Hale Library fire at K-State, a representative from the university's insurance firm flew in from Manhattan every few weeks to meet with library and university staff about cleaning, transport, and disposition of damaged materials (Garcia, 2019). These conversations included multiple campus offices and individuals and communications outside of the university with representatives from insurance and disaster-mitigation contractors.

Project Systems

Colleges and universities employ their own organizational structures, workflows, and policies for physical spaces. Some campuses centralize space and facilities issues, while some rely on a matrix or department-level model. It is important to find out how spaces are designed and maintained prior to beginning a space renovation or design project. There are often dependencies between the individuals and offices required to engage with the project. One office or group may need to approve plans or communicate input before another begins work.

While mapping campus systems and workflows may not feel like a traditional assessment activity, it is essential to understand the space projects complexities in higher education. It is a pre-op activity that can smooth the way for the more traditional space and needs assessments that come later. If new to space design and logistics, start by contacting the facilities director.

Another consideration when assessing project systems' capacity is the timing of the project components. Like offices and individuals, some project elements rely on others to be completed before they begin. For example, stacks must be weeded and cleared before the area can be repurposed. It may be possible to concurrently design a new space while clearing out the old, but the actual renovation work cannot begin until it is empty. It is helpful to break the work down into individual elements to get a better sense of how long each might take to complete, and what resources might be needed or are scarce. This is called a work breakdown structure (WBS) and offers a framework for breaking down and visualizing a project. Each project element or outcome is divided into individual components and mapped based on dependencies and deliverables. A WBS (see figure 11.1) can be simple or complex and often needs to be repeatedly revised throughout a project as

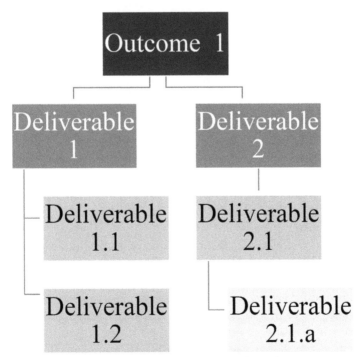

Figure 11.1.   Work Breakdown Structure Template. Pitts

unpredictable issues arise. It can be a helpful tool in developing a logistical plan for the project and identifies where further assessment may be needed to monitor the successful completion of project components.

Space Systems Examples

At CMU, small space adaptations and maintenance are handled by a centralized facilities unit. Larger space redesigns and projects must first pass through the campus design unit, which works with architects and space planners to "study" a space before any contractor or facilities work is started. In cases where hazardous materials like asbestos are present, the health and safety office is involved in the early stages to assess the risk to employees and contractors. Large projects can quickly become complicated and expensive, especially when a design study costs tens of thousands of dollars before any work actually begins.

Consider a space project at CMU where the main library building needed a full-scale renovation. Before the larger renovation began, a significant section of the existing stacks needed to be removed. Before removal, materials on the stacks needed several steps to be weeded. Staff needed to know which items to pull from shelves, which required a usage analysis. When discarding items, carts and boxes were organized and a contract was drafted with a recycling firm to remove weeded items as they were removed from the catalog concurrently. Figure 11.2 offers a partial breakdown of these processes. A WBS can be leveraged in pre-op activities to highlight areas that may benefit from further analysis and assessment, such as print collections assessment.

Structural and Regulatory Considerations

Space projects come in all shapes and sizes. Some are merely cosmetic, requiring only furniture, paint, or other aesthetic decisions that likely do not require much, if any, regulatory oversight. Larger projects, especially those requiring structural changes to a space, involve an internal review before being officially (re)opened to the public. In these cases, a completed pre-op includes a structural assessment inclusive of issues relating to accessibility, building and fire codes, wireless internet capacity, and other infrastructure elements. There may already be documentation on file for the buildings under consideration that offers some structural insights, including key inventories, inspection reports, and fire-suppression maps (a structural element of unique importance in libraries). Beware that many such documents may be lost, dated, incomplete, or nonexistent.

Part of any space assessment pre-op will be the systematic investigation of the records that exist or asking staff and offices that may already have that

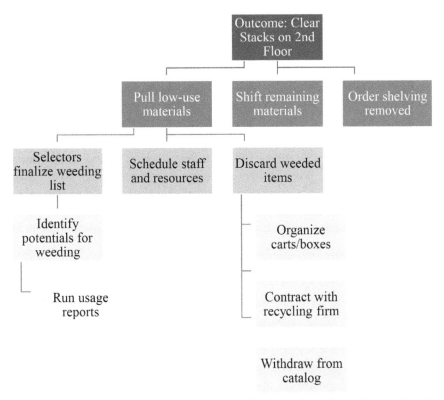

Figure 11.2. Partial Work Breakdown Structure for Carnegie Mellon University Weeding Project. Pitts

structural knowledge to inform the project. Additionally, much literature exists on the nuances of library building considerations, such as the *Checklist of Library Building Design Considerations* (Sannwald, 2016). This and similar volumes offer comprehensive, detailed manuals and accounts of structural considerations in library space development.

Regulatory considerations are also important to understand before conducting any space assessment. Regulatory codes are location- and municipality-specific, and they are sometimes contradictory between agencies. The list of individuals and offices to include on a project team is a good place to start, but having a general understanding of the regulatory workflows will be important to ensure the results of a formal space or needs assessment are not moot from the start. For example, if an area is inaccessible to the public via elevator, it cannot become a major thoroughfare or collaboration area because of the Americans with Disabilities Act (ADA) regulations. There may also be internal or institutional regulations to be aware of, including expense reporting and internal code enforcement.

Leadership in Energy and Environmental Design (LEED) Certification, a program that independently certifies and rates buildings and spaces for sustainable features, is also a structural consideration during a space assessment pre-op. While the merits of environmental certification programs are debated in the larger design community, a space assessment pre-op might gauge the campus and library administration's appetite for sustainable development projects. Meeting LEED certification guidelines or integrating sustainable building practices tend to initially cost more and take longer (Yudelson, 2016). Yet given the cost, time, and energy of building and renovating library spaces, now may be the time to invest in lowering the carbon footprint in the spaces under consideration. Sustainability philosophy should not be an afterthought. Include these discussions in a library space pre-op as a baseline assessment of campus and library willingness to engage resources toward this end.

Structural Examples

CMU's main library building abuts to a large enough thoroughfare to accept medium- to large-sized deliveries, but the design of the dock itself is difficult to navigate with pallet jacks and semi-trucks. Major renovations may require extra planning and even street closures to accommodate construction crews and deliveries. There is also only one elevator for the entire building, which is used for both public and freight transport. Timing and service quality issues come into consideration when a longer-term project is scheduled in higher floors.

The data center for K-State was located in the basement of Hale Library when the 2018 fire occurred (Garcia, 2019). First responders poured hundreds of thousands of gallons of water into the building to stop the fire, most of which wound its way to the basement. Systems went temporarily offline, including university email, student information systems, and a host of other critical digital infrastructure. Accounting for the location of server rooms and other infrastructure not directly related to the roofing project, but potentially impacted by it, was a valuable element of a space assessment pre-op and could have saved time, money, and frustration had efforts been taken to secure the area.

Summary

Major library space building and renovation projects are complex and involve many elements outside most librarians' skillsets. Not only must philosophical and community support issues be assessed, but a basic understanding of the physical spaces and environments they occupy must be reached prior to engagement with designers, contractors, and library decision-makers. A space assessment pre-op helps gain valuable information about spaces and environments before costly barriers and errors are made on the way to new spaces and service infrastructure. Budget capacity should be assessed first and foremost given how expensive building projects can be. Project teams must include the right constellation of stakeholders, campus offices, and facilities personnel who need to be at the table. Systems facilitating infrastructure changes should be catalogued and mapped so that workflow dependencies do not become time-wasting barriers. Finally, structural and regulatory considerations identified ahead of any formal space assessment efficiently rule out ideas that may not be legal or within code requirements. These many facets take time and energy to research, which is why framing the activity via an assessment lens can be helpful for those not versed in the nuances of physical space modifications. A series of pre-op activities results in faster, cheaper, and less frustrating building space assessment and redesign projects.

References

American Library Association. (2014, April 9). *Library construction and renovation.* American Library Association. http://www.ala.org/news/state-americas-libraries-report-2014/library-construction.

Garcia, R. (2019, October 23). After fire and water gut building, Hale Library restoration will likely total $87M. *The Mercury.* https://themercury.com/news/after-fire-and-water-gut-building-hale-library-restoration-will-likely-total-87m/article_36380245-0ea6-57e7-9f88-657f0686ef9d.html.

Marcus, J. (2017, October 10). Why colleges are borrowing billions. *The Atlantic.* https://www.theatlantic.com/education/archive/2017/10/why-colleges-are-borrowing-billions/542352/.

Nitecki, D. (2011). Space assessment as a venue for defining the academic library. *Library Quarterly, 81*(1), 27–59.

Palfrey, J. (2015). *BiblioTech: Why libraries matter more than ever in the age of Google.* Basic Books.

Sannwald, W. W. (2016). *Checklist of library building design considerations* (sixth edition). ALA Editions.

United States Department of Justice. (2012, December 7). *2010 ADA standards for accessible design.* Retrieved from https://www.ada.gov/regs2010/2010ADAStandards/2010ADAstandards.htm.

United States Environmental Protection Agency. (n.d.). *Learn about asbestos.* Retrieved from https://www.epa.gov/asbestos/learn-about-asbestos.

Weiner, S. G. (2005). The history of academic libraries in the United States: A review of the literature. *Library Philosophy and Practice, 7*(2). https://digitalcommons.unl. edu/libphilprac/58/?utm_source=digitalcommons.unl.edu/libphilprac/58&utm_ medium=PDF&utm_campaign=PDFCoverPages.

Yudelson, J. (2016). *Reinventing green building: Why certification systems aren't working and what we can do about it.* New Society Publishers.

Appendix: Space Assessment Pre-Op Template

This template combines the chapter sections that library administrators, assessment coordinators, and space project teams can use.

Table 11.1. Space Assessment Pre-Op Template

Pre-Op Category	Guiding Questions and Considerations	Checklist
Budget	• How much can be allocated to a new space or renovation project this year? Over the next five years? • Has funding for a capital project been requested from central administration? If yes and it was unfunded, why? What can be gleaned to create another, better ask? • Is the project fleshed out enough to pitch to donors? Work with a development officer, if available, to create a pitch. • Can the project be costed out internally? If not, enlist the services of an architect or facilities office.	• Financial review • Historical finance investigation • Campus administration pitch • Donor pitch • Enlist a design firm • Institute savings plan structure • Inflation and materials markup adjustments
Teams	• How will the space teams be structured? • Who should be on each team? • What are the political considerations/ramifications? • How will choose which library staff are involved? • When and how will each team meet? • How will each team report their work?	• Assign project lead • Contacts • Facilities • Campus design • Code enforcement • General counsel • Fire marshall • Access control and security • Human health and safety • Insurance/comptroller • Contracts • Procurement

Pre-Op Category	Guiding Questions and Considerations	Checklist
		• Custodial and waste removal • Sponsored programs • Library and campus stakeholders
Systems	• What systems and workflows are relevant to the project? • What is the progression of engagement for each system? • What are the component parts of each activity and what dependencies are obvious after these are mapped through a WBS? • Keep a facilities log, separate from normal notetaking and documentation efforts, including names, contractors, office numbers, and workflows for easy referral.	• Identify relevant systems • Identify component activities • Map WBS • Create and maintain facilities log • Develop timeline for weekly and monthly WBS assessment and reporting
Structures and Regulations	• What codes and regulations will impact the project? • What offices or individuals enforce regulations on campus? Off campus? • Will LEED certification or other optional environmental factors be considered? • Will the project impact structural systems like HVAC, plumbing, WIFI availability, etc.? • Who can speak on the Library's behalf to regulators and code enforcers? • Where is your IT infrastructure located? • How does IT need to be treated during the project?	Structural documentation to research: • Blueprints or design schematics • Key inventories • Service agreements • Inspection reports • Accessibility accommodation requests • Plumbing and electrical pathway diagrams • Data port and equipment installations records • Security measures and access control protocols • Loading dock and elevator access • Fire suppression maps and triggers

~

CHAPTER TWELVE

Facilitating Innovative Research, Creative Thinking, and Problem-Solving

A Collaborative Assessment Framework

Laura I. Spears, PhD, Adrian P. Del Monte,
Jean L. Bossart, Valrie Minson, Jason Meneely, PhD,
Margaret Portillo, PhD, Sara Russell Gonzalez, PhD,
Sheila J. Bosch, PhD, University of Florida

Between 2014 and 2017, the Marston Science Library (MSL) of the University of Florida (UF) George A. Smathers Libraries renovated three of its five floors, creating new public spaces that included a visualization conference room with geographic information systems (GIS) and informatics tools, technology-enhanced quiet study areas, a virtual reality lab, and a makerspace. These renovations provided MSL the opportunity to host annual hackathons and support other events, such as the Girls Tech Camp and a middle school technology camp designed to facilitate creative thinking and problem-solving. With two more floors needing renovations, the MSL team was interested in better understanding how the renovations may support innovative, interdisciplinary research as well as promote creative thinking and problem-solving in the student population.

In September 2018, the Association of Research Libraries initiated the "Research Library Impact: Pilot Models for Scalable and Sustainable Assessment" for libraries to explore research questions of great importance to academic libraries. The MSL team explored how library spaces facilitate innovative research, creative thinking, and problem-solving. To add expertise in learning environment design, the MSL team collaborated with researchers from the UF Department of Interior Design (IND). The UF IND was awarded an ASID Foundation Transform Grant to conduct research that advances knowledge on how the interior environment shapes human experience. The study examined a range of learning zones within the built environment on university campuses (Bosch, 2016). This project received a 2018 Environmental Design Research Association Certificate of Environmental Excellence Award. With a view toward renovating the remaining two floors, the MSL-IND team examined ways the current library space design facilitates innovative, interdisciplinary research, creative thinking, and problem-solving.

The MSL-IND team implemented a mixed-method study that included:

- a full spatial analysis of space allocated for each of four dimensions (together vs. individual and public vs. private) to identify building capabilities;
- an intercept survey utilizing an adjective checklist designed to elicit student perceptions of existing space and desired/ideal spaces; and
- focus groups of students and employees designed to validate the adjective checklist survey results.

This chapter presents the study's methodology along with the first intercept survey results to inform other libraries performing an analysis of their own space usage and design.

Literature Review

Examining Library Spaces

Up until the 1990s, the motivation for library design focused on maximizing space to house ever-growing physical collections; however, that changed with the introduction of digital collections. Digital formats freed librarians to rethink their physical spaces to focus more on optimizing student learning experiences. Consequently, the library paradigm shifted from book-centered library spaces emphasizing individual study to learning-centered environments with group study areas (Bennett, 2007).

Students primarily perceive the academic library as a learning and information place, using the library for individual and group study, finding information, computer use, reference services, meetings, and socializing. They perceive their academic library as a multipurpose destination (Kim, 2017). Recent studies of student library use showed two distinct user groups of academic libraries: those who come for individual study and those students who meet at the library for collaborative study, with both groups having specific requirements and using the library in different ways (Khoo et al., 2016).

To understand how students study and use library spaces, researchers often use surveys and focus groups. For a recent library renovation at an Ohio university, the library conducted student and faculty focus groups and a survey (Baril and Kobiela, 2017). The results indicated that students frequently work in groups, which is an integral part of their learning. Because many students switch between individual study and group study, libraries need to offer flexible spaces with multiple uses. For academic libraries to understand how their spaces are used by students, it is helpful for libraries to conduct a space audit to determine how students use specific spaces (Bieraugel and Neill, 2017).

Renovating an existing library space incurs a large capital expense, so it is important to consider the preferences and behavior of students. Incorporation of a variety of furniture types leverages the advantages of these flexible floor plans, allowing students to decide where and how to study within each zone (Kim et al., 2020).

The emergence of COVID-19 in early 2020 drove library patrons to use more online resources and to spend less in-person time within the physical library. In response, academic libraries quickly reinvented their services and collection access to support the new blended learning environment (Sukula et al., 2020). It may be several years before it is clear whether these trends evolve into a long-term paradigm shift.

Individual, Group, Public, Private Framework

Libraries long considered public/private and individual/group zones as one and the same, but research suggests that a campus library should be developed to clearly support independent work within a public setting or collaborative work in a private setting (Kim et al., 2020). This study builds on Kim et al.'s systematic research process of unobtrusive observation of student behavior in the space combined with a survey, conducted online and face-to-face, within the MSL library branch. The study focused on functional, environmental, social, and psychological needs. Key results indicated that students heavily use individual bench seating with dividers; group seating analysis found that users "were more likely to choose seats with linear arrangements, rather than those with round arrangements" (Kim et al., 2020, p. 4). In addition, Kim et al.'s findings acknowledged students' nuanced views of the value of noise in a space, as a challenge but also a feature that provides a sense of togetherness resulting from "a dialectical interplay between students' desire to be alone and their desire to be with others" (p. 8).

Toward Place-based Markers of Library Environments

What has been well-established in the literature is that people are readily able to express definite preferences about physical environments frequented in daily life. The present study drew on a well-established assessment method for understanding defining characteristics of the creative person to develop a human-centered method for measuring end-user perceptions of the built environment. Specifically, the Adjective Checklist (ACL), developed by Gough and Heilbrun in the mid-sixties and later expanded to include widely used creative personality subscales (Domino, 1970; Gough, 1979), was useful in operationalizing the place-based semantic differential created for the present study.

Gough's ACL required respondents to select from three hundred adjectives that best define their core personality. For the place-based assessment developed for the present study, pairs of contrasting adjectives (i.e., semantic differential scale) gauge end-user impressions of library spaces. Conceptualizing these spaces using adjectives or place-based descriptors on a continuum, rather than a binary concept, proved useful in creating a more nuanced understanding of the social and physical space qualities.

Students independently rated a particular library space using fifteen place-based adjective pairs designed to capture perceptions of specific library floors. These place-based adjectives created a framework upon which to elaborate further during subsequent student and staff focus groups.

System-wide Diversity

The ability for space to be highly adaptable to individual and institutional, as well as normative and non-normative, factors is critical to creating a system supporting problem-solving, creativity, and satisfaction. A vibrant place-based ecology is diverse and adaptable. These environments accommodate ways of working individually and in groups; they offer technology-infused ways of studying and working and address the whole person, who needs to concentrate, take breaks, work with others, or locate and retrieve materials.

This approach requires a heightened awareness of system-wide diversity and a systemic understanding of people and place. This creative ecology has been mapped out for the workplace and holds true for successfully adapting to the systemic challenges facing the university research library (Portillo and Meneely, 2015). How does the library retain its core identity, mission, and its centrality within the academy, while adapting its practices and physical spaces to create safe, supportive, and vibrant environments for diverse individuals and groups? We maintain that these challenges can be negotiated to creatively adapt library environments to support social distancing within pandemic realities and can reinforce or reshape the place of the library on the campus to offer a resilient and engaging environment.

Methods

The study was conducted in two phases at the MSL. Phase 1 included a spatial analysis and an intercept survey. Phase 2 (conducted in spring 2021 and not reported here) will include four student focus groups and one employee focus group with prompts derived from the intercept survey.

Spatial Analysis

A spatial analysis of the existing work environment documented the intended (and pre-pandemic) use of the current workspace. Existing spaces were categorized into one of four categories: individual-public, individual-private; group-public, and group-private.

Integral to the study was to examine how students utilize the space and how spatial attributes and adjacencies might best support both the independent and collaborative work needs of the students and staff in these four types of zones.

The individual-public zone (figure 12.1 A) is characterized as a flexible space for individual use that is located in a communal area designed for more collaborative work. Often, a partition provides a demarcation, yet allows users to be seen, connect with their surroundings, and switch between individual and group user preferences.

The individual-private zone (figure 12.1 B) is generally a quiet environment that visually isolates users from its surroundings. Examples are study carrels and quiet rooms for solitary use.

The group-public zone (figure 12.1 C) is a communal workspace that supports diverse group sizes for social and collaborative activities. This zone includes lounges and other types of inbetween spaces that fall outside traditional use of libraries (cafeterias, coffee shops, etc.).

The group-private zone (figure 12.1 D) is a fully or partially enclosed space designed for group usage within a communal area; a makeshift partition like a mobile white board quickly differentiates the space.

To assess the usage of the physical environment within the MSL, data was collected through a cross-sectional observational study of users engaging in a specific type of activity over a focused time period. The emphasis documented how users utilized the library space based on the individual-group and public-private library zones framework. A visual sweep of the entire

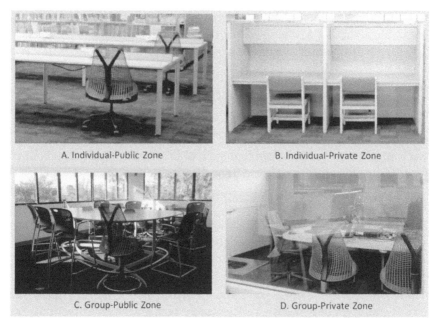

A. Individual-Public Zone

B. Individual-Private Zone

C. Group-Public Zone

D. Group-Private Zone

Figure 12.1. Examples of Spatial Analysis Zones in Marston Science Library. Spears et al.

floor was conducted to record users' activity and furniture utilization (see appendix A).

The user's activity and furniture utilization illustrate MSL occupancy, groupings, and spaces. Although the library's open spaces provide seating options for individual and group utilization, users preferred studying or working individually regardless of furniture and seating type. Heavy traffic and crowding were observed on the first three floors, where communal and collaborative settings are accessible and have recently been renovated. Alternatively, the designated quiet spaces, where most students utilize the space for studying alone, are available on the uppermost floors.

Intercept Survey

The intercept survey collected student preferences related to the four use categories (private, public, group, individual), fourteen space categories, and three system-wide diversity factors, asking students to define existing spaces using a place-based semantic differential (PBSD), as shown in appendix B. The PBSD scale was offered twice, first focusing on the user's perception of the current MSL spaces and second focusing on spaces the user might consider as ideal. Drawing on design methodologies, the two PBSD questions included visual prompts comprising images of the current library spaces as well as images of other academic libraries from around the world. Additional open-ended questions were used to solicit the user's perceptions of the space they "typically use" in their own words and their ideas for potential future renovations to the MSL.

Initially the study sought to recruit library patrons using a location-based, convenience sample approach. However, the COVID-19 social-distancing requirements reduced the number of students on campus and responses to the survey using in-library signage were meager. Thus, the survey recruitment shifted to an online questionnaire distribution to the entire student population. To address the problem of recall bias, images of the MSL were inserted into the survey as memory aids; also, the survey controlled for participants who had never visited the library in person.

Preliminary Findings

The online survey was distributed November 9–21, 2020, with 544 responding to the survey. Of these respondents, sixty-three had never visited MSL. After removing incomplete data and respondents who have not yet visited MSL, the data remaining for analysis comprises 337 completed surveys distributed across all sixteen of the university's colleges. The analysis shows that 82.4 percent of respondents were undergraduates (n = 277), and 17 percent were graduates (n = 57), with two responses provided by professional or other categories. The general UF student population comprises 68.9 percent undergraduates, 22.6 percent graduates, and 8.5 percent professional or other students. Respondents primarily represent five colleges, including engineering (n = 84), liberal arts and sciences (n = 78), agriculture and life sciences (n = 56), business (n = 43), and design, construction, and planning (n = 15). Selected for discussion are the users' reported library usage, responses to the ranking, and the comments provided regarding the respondents' desires for future renovations for MSL.

Reported Library Usage

The MSL comprises five floors, with entry to the building located on the second floor. The basement was renovated in the past seven years to become a "commons" space with a combination of group and individual study spaces, a classroom, a meeting room, and a computer lab, but no materials shelving. The second and third floors are also collaborative study floors, with the fourth and fifth floors designated as quiet and silent study floors, respectively. Sixty percent of respondents (n = 201) typically use the basement and the third-floor spaces. Twenty-four percent of respondents indicate they typically use the fourth and fifth floors of MSL. Interestingly, over 56 percent of undergraduate respondents use the top three floors, while over 57 percent of graduate students use the basement and entry level floors. This finding challenges the assumption that undergraduates only want more so-cial, commons-designed areas, and that graduate students are solely seeking quiet, individual spaces in which to work. However, when asked about the frequency of usage for specific tasks using a five-point Likert scale, under-graduate students reported higher average rankings of group study (average 2.7) than graduate students (average 2.2). More typically though, their time spent socializing (undergraduate average of 2.1 vs. graduate average of 1.6) and "taking a break/passing time" (undergraduate average of 2.5 vs. graduate average of 2.1) were higher than those of graduate students. In fact, 66.7 percent of graduate students report "rarely" socializing at the library, whereas 35.7 percent of undergraduates report socializing twice a month to up to four times per week.

Place-based Semantic Differential (PBSD)
Respondents graded the PBSD using a five-point Likert scale (Strongly Pleasant = 1, Slightly Pleasant = 2, Neutral = 3, Slightly Unpleasant = 4, and Strongly Unpleasant = 5). Means under 3 favored the first term and means over 3 favored the second term. The means for the set of adjectives based on current use indicate that respondents perceive the current MSL as more serious than playful, calm rather than energetic, arousing rather than sleepy, more unsocial than social, less collaborative than self-reliant, gloomier, and uncrowded. Students overall were neutral about noise and formality but scored the MSL as more friendly, public, authentic, relaxing, and pleasant (see table 12.1). However, students' ideal space would be even less crowded ($\Delta = 1.1$), more arousing ($\Delta = 0.9$), more exciting ($\Delta = 0.7$), more friendly ($\Delta = 0.6$), and more collaborative ($\Delta = 0.5$).

Examining these findings by class status, results indicate similar desires for an ideal space to be more arousing, collaborative, social, and relaxing; however, undergraduates reported stronger feelings about the need for social spaces (m = 2.5 vs. 2.8) and greater privacy (m = 2.6 vs. 2.5) than graduates. Graduates indicated stronger scores for arousing and exciting spaces and for more collaborative (m = 2.2 vs. 2.4) but quieter (m = 1.9 vs. 2.1) spaces. Thus, undergraduates are seeking both more privacy with less emphasis on collaboration than graduate students, who are seeking collaborative and more exciting but quiet spaces.

Table 12.1. Means for Place-based Semantic Differential Adjectives

Adjectives	Index	Total (n = 334)	Undergraduate	Graduate
(1) Public/Private (5)	Current	2.3	2.4	2.1
	Ideal	2.6	2.6	2.5
(1) Sleepy/Arousing (5)	Current	2.9	2.9	3.1
	Ideal	3.8	3.8	3.9
(1) Exciting/Gloomy (5)	Current	2.9	2.9	2.8
	Ideal	2.2	2.2	2.1
(1) Crowded/Uncrowded	Current	2.7	2.7	2.9
(5)	Ideal	3.8	3.8	3.9
(1) Friendly/Unfriendly (5)	Current	2.3	2.3	2.3
	Ideal	1.7	1.7	1.6
(1) Collaborative/Self-	Current	2.9	2.9	2.8
Reliant (5)	Ideal	2.4	2.4	2.2
(1) Social/Unsocial (5)	Current	2.9	2.9	2.9
	Ideal	2.6	2.5	2.8
(1) Relaxing/Distressing (5)	Current	2.2	2.2	2.4
	Ideal	1.7	1.7	1.8
(1) Energetic/Calm (5)	Current	3.1	3.1	2.9
	Ideal	2.9	2.9	2.8
(1) Playful/Serious (5)	Current	3.4	3.4	3.4
	Ideal	3.1	3.1	3.2
(1) Informal/Formal (5)	Current	2.5	2.5	2.4
	Ideal	2.5	2.5	2.6
(1) Pleasant/Unpleasant (5)	Current	1.8	1.7	1.9
	Ideal	1.3	1.3	1.3
(1) Authentic/Superficial (5)	Current	2.3	2.3	2.4
	Ideal	1.8	1.8	2.0
(1) Quiet/Noisy (5)	Current	2.5	2.4	2.7
	Ideal	2.1	2.1	1.9

Analyzing all adjectives using a Chi square test for association, a weak, statistically significant association occurred between the respondent's class and their responses on the Relaxed/Distressed adjectives $X^2 = (4, n = 334) = 10.68$, $p < .05$, indicating that graduate students still perceived ideal spaces as distressing, as opposed to few undergraduates who did.

To examine the value of the PBSD instrument for use in this study, Cronbach's Alpha test for reliability was conducted on both the current PBSD (Cronbach alpha = .749) and the ideal PBSD (Cronbach alpha = .738). There was only one inter-item correlation that met the acceptable threshold of .70 between the Social/Unsocial and the Playful/Serious adjectives (Cronbach alpha = .708). While the items meet the threshold for reliability, further testing is indicated to determine inter-item correlation.

Students' Desires for Renovations

One question collected comments from users about desired future renovations to the MSL resulting in a total of 636 codes that were distributed into three concepts: space concept (n = 267), system-wide diversity (n = 240), and use concept (n = 129). Codes are in appendix C.

The comments were analyzed for their relationship to the ideal PBSD scale and to their relationship to class status (i.e., undergraduate, graduate). The space concept codes and system-wide diversity codes both resulted in statistically significant relationships to class status, with undergraduates describing 83.8 percent of the space features, while graduates described only 16.2 percent (Pearson X^2 (1, n = 352) = 17.17, p < .05); while 83.9 percent of system-wide diversity codes were provided by undergraduates and graduates provided just 16.1 percent (Pearson X^2 (1, n = 352) = 11.57, p < .05). Both relationships, however, were weak as indicated by the Phi metric, which was .221 for the space concept and .181 for system-wide diversity. Ideal PBSC scale significantly associated with the comment codes include Playful/Serious, Social/Unsocial, and Friendly/Unfriendly (see table 12.2).

Table 12.2. Relationship of Comments to the Ideal PBSD

Comment Concept	PBSD Adjective Pair	Pearson Chi-Square			Phi	
		Value	df	Significance	Value	Significance*
System-wide Diversity	Playful/Serious	9.75	4	.045	.171	.045
System-wide Diversity	Social/Unsocial	9.98	4	.041	.173	.041
Space	Playful/Serious	12.18	4	.016	.191	.016
Space	Social/Unsocial	8.50	4	.075	.159	.075
Private (Use)	Friendly/ Unfriendly	10.02	4	.040	.173	.040

* (P < .05)

In the case of the system-wide diversity relationships with the ideal adjectives, in both cases, the comments for Playful/Serious and Social/Unsocial were stronger in the midranges (Slightly-Neutral-Slightly), indicating that students desire spaces that can satisfy both a playful and serious environment and provide opportunities for both social and unsocial needs. The space concept relationships with these same two variables exhibited the same results, with greater concentration of scores on the same two ideal adjectives in the midranges. For the use concept, the factors were analyzed separately, with the private factor relationship with the ideal adjectives, Friendly/Unfriendly, as the only statistically significant relationship indicated.

The survey results merit more statistical testing; also, given the indications of a tension between the Playful/Serious and Social/Unsocial adjectives, operationalizing these scores through further analysis of their associated comments and in the focus groups would develop the specific characteristics of desired ideal spaces.

Summary and Next Steps

The spatial analysis revealed patterns in how libraries are designed, including occupancy counts, number of students studying, and spaces they are using. Looking toward the future, the findings of this spatial analysis inform future renovation plans of the MSL's fourth and fifth floors.

The survey confirmed the use of a place-based semantic differential for investigation of how students feel about library spaces and generated key findings about the existence of system-wide diversity tension and spaces that offer both social/unsocial and playful/serious spaces. Also, graduate students are using floors that are more "commons-oriented," thereby louder and more crowded. This conflicts with their results on desired quiet and serious spaces but would complement their scores on increased collaborative spaces. Although study carrels are often located in more quiet areas of a library, while group study rooms tend to be in noisier, more social locations, a high proportion of students observed in group-oriented spaces were studying independently. Today's college students expect to "have choices and control those choices" (Singleton-Jackson et al., 2010, p. 346). Our results may indicate that ideal library spaces provide diverse choices that can be controlled in the moment of need by the student, as noted by Cunningham and Tabur (2012). The floor usage and intercept survey results, in conjunction with the student and faculty focus groups, will be used to design these floors to complement the other three and ensure that patrons have access to the types of space and resources that they need for studying, research, innovation, and collaboration.

References

Association of Research Libraries (2018, September). *Research library impact pilots.* Association of Research Libraries. https://www.arl.org/research-library-impact-pilots-2/.

Baril, K., and Kobiela, K. (2017). Reimagining the library: Designing spaces to meet the needs of today's students. *Scholarship and Practice of Undergraduate Research,* *1*(2), 18–23. https://doi.org/http://dx.doi.org/10.18833/spur/1/2/9.

Bennett, S. (2007). Designing for uncertainty: Three approaches. *The Journal of Academic Librarianship, 33*(2), 169–75.

Bieraugel, M., and Neill, S. (2017). Ascending Bloom's pyramid: Fostering student creativity and innovation in academic library spaces. *College and Research Libraries, 78*(1), 35–52. https://doi.org/https://doi.org/10.5860/crl.78.1.35.

Bosch, S. J. (2016). *Mixed-use learning zones: A typology for bridging learning from the academe to the profession.* ASID transform grant. College of Design, Construction and Planning University of Florida. Retrieved January 22, 2021. https://dcp.ufl.edu/interior/asid-transform-grant/.

Cunningham, H. V., and Tabur, S. (2012). Learning space attributes: Reflections on academic library design and its use. *Journal of Learning Spaces, 1*(2), 1–6.

Domino, G. (1970). Identification of potentially creative persons from the Adjective Check List. *Journal of Consulting and Clinical Psychology, 35*(10), 48–51. https://doi.org/10.1037/h0029624.

Gough, H. G. (1979). A creativity personality scale for the Adjective Check List. *Journal of Personality and Social Psychology, 37*(8), 1398–405. https://psycnet.apa.org/doi/10.1037/0022-3514.37.8.1398.

Khoo, M. J., Rozaklis, L., Hall, C., and Kusunoki, D. (2016). "A really nice spot": Evaluating place, space, and technology in academic libraries. *College and Research Libraries, 77*(1), 51–70.

Kim, D., Bosch, S., and Lee, J. H. (2020). Alone with others: Understanding physical environmental needs of students within an academic library setting. *The Journal of Academic Librarianship, 46*(2), 1–9. https://doi.org/https://doi.org/10.1016/j.acalib.2019.102098.

Kim, J.-A. (2017). User perception and use of the academic library: A correlation analysis. *The Journal of Academic Librarianship, 43*(3), 49–53.

Portillo, M., and Meneely, J. (2015). Toward a creative ecology of workplace design. In J. Asher Thompson and N. Blossom (Eds.), *The handbook of interior design* (pp. 112–27). Wiley-Blackwell.

Singleton-Jackson, J. A., Jackson, D. L., and Reinhardt, J. (2010). Students as consumers of knowledge: Are they buying what we're selling? *Innovative Higher Education, 35*(5), 343–58.

Sukula, S. K., Thapa, N., Kumar, M., and Awasthi, S. (2020). Reinventing academic libraries and learning–post-COVID (19) in the perspective of collaboration among key stake-holders in higher education: A brief assessment and futuristic approach. *International Journal of Research in Library Science, 6*(1), 77.

Appendix A: Layout Used in Spatial Analysis

On specific days of the week, the user's location and activity were observed and recorded within the fifteen-minute timeframe, twice during the day and in the evening. The schedule was determined based on the peak hours of a three-year traffic data of library operation. The activity was repli-

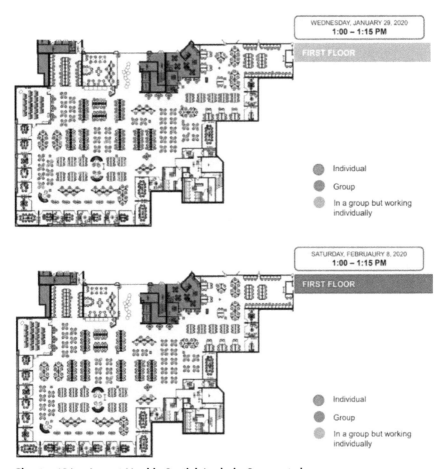

Chapter 12A. Layout Used in Spatial Analysis. Spears et al.

cated throughout all five floors of the library for four weeks from January to February 2020.

Appendix B: Survey with
Place-based Semantic Differential Scales

This survey asks you to evaluate the existing space you typically work in at Marston Science Library. You will be asked how the existing spaces make you feel as well as how they ideally should function. Important note: This survey is about your perceptions; therefore, there are no right or wrong answers. This survey should take no longer than twelve minutes to complete.

Q1. Have you ever used the Marston Science Library in person? (Yes, No, Not yet)

Q2. Please indicate which floor of the Marston Science Library you typically use:

(skips to the relevant question based on response)

(Basement, Entry level, Third floor, Fourth floor, Fifth Floor)

Q3a. Please describe how you feel about the space when working on the basement floor of Marston Library.

Q3b. Please describe how you feel about the space when working on the entry floor of Marston Library.

Q3c. Please describe how you feel about the space when working on the third floor of Marston Library.

Q3d. Please describe how you feel about the space when working on the fourth floor of Marston Library.

Q3e. Please describe how you feel about the space when working on the fifth floor of Marston Library.

Q4. Please elaborate on what specific characteristics of the space contribute to your answer above. (Please be as descriptive as possible.)

Q5. If you could change anything about this floor of Marston Library, what would it be? (Please be as descriptive as possible.)

Q6. For each of the following adjective pairs, please respond to the statement by checking the box in the appropriate column. The current space of Marston Science Library that I typically work in feels . . .

	Strongly 1	Slightly 2	Neutral 3	Slightly 4	Strongly 5	
Pleasant						Unpleasant
Relaxing						Distressing
Sleepy						Arousing
Exciting						Gloomy
Energetic						Calm
Quiet						Noisy
Playful						Serious
Social						Unsocial
Collaborative						Self-Reliant
Public						Private
Informal						Formal
Authentic						Superficial
Friendly						Unfriendly
Crowded						Uncrowded

Q7. For each of the following adjective pairs please respond to the statement by checking the box in the appropriate column. Ideally, I wish this space of Marston Science Library would be:

	Strongly 1	Slightly 2	Neutral 3	Slightly 4	Strongly 5	
Pleasant						Unpleasant
Relaxing						Distressing
Sleepy						Arousing
Exciting						Gloomy
Energetic						Calm
Quiet						Noisy
Playful						Serious
Social						Unsocial
Collaborative						Self-Reliant
Public						Private
Informal						Formal
Authentic						Superficial
Friendly						Unfriendly
Crowded						Uncrowded

Q8. If we were to renovate the Marston Science Library, what improvements would you like to see made?

Q9. How often have you used the Marston Science Library for the following tasks?

Tasks: Team Projects, Group Study, Individual Work/Study, Socializing, Taking a Break/Passing Time, Other—Please describe.

Frequency: Very frequently (more than four times weekly), Frequently (one or two times weekly), Infrequently (one or two times monthly), Intermittently (as needed to complete coursework/research), Rarely (once in a blue moon).

Q10. How frequently have COVID-19 distancing changes limited your ability to perform the following task?

Tasks: Team Projects, Group Study, Individual Work/Study, Socializing, Taking a Break/Passing Time, Other—Please describe.

Frequency: Very frequently (more than four times weekly), Frequently (one to two times weekly), Infrequently (one to two times monthly), Intermittently (as needed to complete coursework/research), Rarely (once in a blue moon).

Q11. In light of the social-distancing measures in place in response to the COVID-19 pandemic, how do you feel about the Marston Library spaces? (Like, Neutral, Dislike)

Q12. How many hours per week do you typically spend at the Marston Science Library?
(less than an hour, two to four hours, five to seven hours, eight to ten hours, eleven or more hours)

Q13. Please select your class status:
(Undergraduate, Graduate, Professional, Other—Please describe)

Q14. Please select your college:

Q15. Please indicate your major:

Q16. Please list your year of birth:

Appendix C: Codebook for Question Responses

Space Concept	System-wide Diversity	Use Concept
Aesthetics	Anti-establishment	Group
Ambiance	Establishment	Individual
Amenities	Mixed (establishment/anti-establishment)	Private
Architectural		Public
Building Features		
Color		
Comfort		
Component		
Fenestration		
Functionality		
Furnishings		
In-between Spaces		
Lighting		
Materials		
Unknown		
Wayfinding		

~

CHAPTER THIRTEEN

Personnel Relationship Assessments

Holt Zaugg

Personnel relationship assessments are perhaps the most difficult assessments to conduct and disseminate because they specifically talk about library employees, their actions, and the ways in which findings are acted upon. Typically, these assessments are only for library employees, as they examine the professional interactions between library employees that facilitate how things are done behind the scenes. These assessments represent the confluence of a variety of employee issues and the corresponding emotional responses. Before delving further into personnel relationship assessments, it is important to define what these assessments are not and what they are. Personnel relationship assessments are not used for end-of-year, rank advancement, or pay-increase evaluations. They are not personal relationship assessments that seek to "correct" an employee's behavior or perceived character flaws. Those types of evaluations are left to a supervisor, library leadership, or the individual who seeks to improve her- or himself.

Personnel relationship assessments examine how library employees interact with and among each other in the discharge of their assigned duties. The assessments primarily examine the employee actions as a group to determine better ways to interact and complete job tasks. When doing so, they examine inequalities based in ethnicity, gender, university status, or some other demographic category. They seek to understand and emulate patterns of behavior that contribute to strong and effective organizations. These assessments may focus on such things as communication patterns or networks, collaboration skills, professional development effectiveness, compensation, or activities that increase the efficacy and collegiality within the organization.

Many institutions require assessment approval from their institutional review board (IRB) prior to dissemination. While it is an extra step, an IRB review examines the assessment with a second set of eyes to identify any problematic areas. Whether personnel relationship assessments are disseminated beyond the university or not, an IRB review is essential to prevent harm to employees.

Often these assessments examine personnel relationships on a state, national, or international level, but the root of personnel relationship assessments is within each library. These assessments may involve two or more departments or the entire library, but their benefit is seen in the level of employee interactions. They are most effective when employees' perspective and understanding is enlarged, allowing them to change and improve the way they complete their job tasks.

The difficulty with these types of assessments arises when employees have ingrained biases and fixed actions that prevent them from improving how things are done. An additional layer of complexity arises when a library employee is tasked with collecting and analyzing potentially sensitive data about their colleagues' experiences. This chapter discusses some considerations to keep in mind when conducting assessments of library personnel relationships using the four assessment tasks outlined in chapter 1.

Design

In addition to the typical design features necessary for any assessment, there are some special considerations for personnel relationship assessments. Personnel relationship assessments often occur at the national or international level as they examine specific issues. Galbraith et al. (2018) and Silva and Galbraith (2018) examined issues surrounding employee compensation, specifically gaps in salary compensation sorted by gender and ethnic background and differences in the ways different genders negotiated compensation and how successful they were. While both of these studies examined human resources (HR) issues at a national level, the issues are also relevant at a local level, and the methodology used can be adapted to an individual library. At the local level, compensation and negotiation patterns could be explored to determine any differences. The larger assessment can serve as a model for a local assessment; however, there are several assessment design issues that need to be addressed to complete a successful local personnel relationship assessment.

Scope

Scope determines the parameters of data collection—what will and will not be included in the assessment. The temptation is to extend the assessment beyond its original parameters because it may be the only chance evaluators have to ask employees about personnel relationship issues or because the assessment has different layers of complexity that are not a typical part of assessments. A clear delineation of the scope of the assessment prevents scope creep and provides a clear focus for the assessment. Evaluators need the discipline to reject efforts for additional data collection that would further confound any given assessment.

Representation

Personnel from each group examined in the assessment need to be involved in the planning of the assessment. Depending on the purpose of the assessment, these groups are determined based on a variety of demographics, such as gender, ethnicity, employment status, length of library employment, and education or training, to name a few. Providing fair representation from each group in the assessment planning ensures a voice for each group. It enables those designing the assessment to see things from a different perspective. For example, if an assessment centers on gender equity in the library, representatives from all genders employed in the library should be included. This ensures that perspectives from each group are considered in the planning.

Influence

The assessment should also avoid the perception of influence by any one group. If there are trust issues between library leadership and the rank-and-file employees, steps may need to be taken to prevent real or perceived library leadership influence during the assessment. Similarly, if there is a dominant ethnic group, care needs to be taken so that group does not override the perspectives of minority groups. If an employee is known to have strong feelings or perspectives that may influence the design of the assessment, she or he should not be on the committee that plans and conducts the assessment, but she or he should be invited to participate in the assessment. This allows her or his perspectives to be heard but not skew the way the assessment is conducted.

The assessment needs to be conducted more openly and transparently than usual. Evaluators need to schedule information sessions to explain the plan and adjust it to address any concerns. These sessions are preceded or followed by emails, newsletters, or other personalized explanations of the assessment for those unable to attend the information sessions. If the assessment examines an issue that is particularly sensitive, it may be best to engage outside assessment personnel to conduct the assessment.

Leadership Support

The assessment team should ask for and receive the support of leadership at all levels of the library. If the assessment involves two or three departments, the respective department chairs should fully support and promote the assessment. Similar support should occur with divisional and full library leadership for assessments at those levels. Sometimes this support involves financial incentives, such as on-the-clock participation during data collection or monetary incentives for participating. The support of leaders indicates the importance of the assessment to those in their line of supervision. Leadership can help explain the importance of the assessment and offer encouragement for employees to participate without trying to influence how they respond in data collection. Leadership support is also critical in following up with and acting on assessment findings.

Confidentiality and Privacy

The design of personnel relationship assessments needs to have additional levels of confidentiality and privacy. If these provisions are not in place, employees may be reluctant to openly express their feelings and discuss their experiences out of fear of reprisals. Consideration should be given to raising the level of confidentiality to that of anonymity. The difference between the two levels is that of knowing but safeguarding participants' identities and not knowing participants' identities.

Data Collection

There are four types of assessment tools that are uniquely suited to personnel relationships assessments. These assessment tools do not represent all possible data-collection methods, but they are well suited to personnel relationship assessments.

Surveys

A key difference with personnel relationship assessment surveys is that they typically use a population instead of a sample, allowing all employees to participate in the assessment. Cross and Parker (2004) used population-based surveys to determine social networks within business organizations. Detailed surveys were sent to all members within defined groups asking about the level of interactions that promote communication and collaborations within the organization. The result was a network showing individuals who were well connected to others, individuals who were bottlenecks in the organization, and individuals who were isolated. While most of Cross and Parker's (2004) work was done with businesses, similar surveys can be used within a library to show communication and collaboration networks that provide insights on how to improve task completion. In this type of assessment, employees will need to be identified for the assessment to have its full impact.

Interviews/Focus Groups

Interviews and focus groups provide in-depth and detailed information that explains why something is happening. They are conducted in a similar manner as explained in previous chapters, including audio or video recordings for accuracy. If the assessment is of a sensitive nature, these recordings easily identify the participant, so extra precautions need to be taken, such as having an outside evaluator conduct the interview or focus group and providing a deidentified transcript for analysis. For an added layer of privacy, the external reviewer may complete the analysis and provide a summary report that does not identify specific individuals. This extra layer of confidentiality helps participants speak freely about their experiences and be assured that their comments will be kept confidential.

In planning focus groups for one sensitive personnel relationship assessment, the assessment librarian used an external evaluator and provided guidelines whereby focus groups were created by gender and supervisors were not in the same focus group as supervised employees. Since the focus group room was in the Assessment Department offices, the assessment librarian left his office fifteen minutes prior to the focus group and did not return until fifteen minutes following the focus group. These actions allowed participants to arrive at and leave the focus group without being identified. Although the focus groups were video recorded for accuracy, the external interviewer provided deidentified transcripts for analysis by another external evaluator. These design features prevented anyone on the assessment team from knowing who participated in the focus group or what was said. This open and transparent step indicated the researchers' desire to maintain the privacy and anonymity of those participating.

Process Flow Charts

Gifts to the library have a specialized route, as the library determines if the gift is needed or wanted for their collection all the way through making it accessible to patrons. At one library a flow chart helped special collections curators, catalogers, and others join together to describe the process from accepted donation to accessible resource. The discussion helped increase the understanding of what others in the library did and how they could help each other.

The creation and revision of process flow charts provides the opportunity for library employees with interconnected tasks to communicate better. It helps understanding of the entire process instead of focusing on siloed activities. It also is a means to build trust among employees.

Case Studies

One example of a case study would be the examination of trends in employee compensation over time and between genders. While this is not a communication issue, it is an examination of an equity issue. The compensation data already exists and can be easily accessed by those with permission to determine how compensation has changed or needs to change. Care should also be taken to ensure individual privacy.

Another case study may examine the communication patterns among library employees. The form of communication (face-to-face, telephone, text, email, etc.), the level of frequency (never, as needed, or on a periodic basis), and intensity (quick informative communication to a deep, intense conversation) would help employees determine if they are communicating at the proper level, frequency, and degree of intensity that they should be. Such a case study can be conducted with a survey to all library employees and it may include follow-up interviews.

Data Analysis

Personnel relationship assessments follow established protocols for quantitative and qualitative data analysis but with a heightened awareness of and actions ensuring privacy and confidentiality. Process flow charts and case studies have a built-in iterative component that allows them to be repeatedly reviewed during the process and periodically after completion. It is helpful to have an individual who has experience creating process flow charts guide the development process.

Dissemination

Dissemination should occur within the library or library units associated with the assessment and, depending on the assessment, to associated university leadership. Findings may also be presented in peer-reviewed publications or conferences, but results should be presented in aggregate with no individual being identified. Following the release of results, library leadership and employees need to develop and implement a comprehensive plan of action for implementing change. Dissemination for personnel relationship assessments has a more detailed follow-up plan because of its direct connection to library employees.

Value and Decision-Making

Unlike other categories of assessments, personnel relationship assessments focus on the interactions among library employees. While they are not intended for evaluation, promotion, or rank-advancement purposes, these assessments do provide opportunities for library employees to do things better. A comprehensive, collaborative effort to implement the assessment findings is necessary. The leadership style may vary but should match with library employees as decisions on how to proceed with the assessment findings are made.

Wilson (2017) described how collaborative leadership facilitates such an effort by helping library employees know the community they collaborate with better as they pursue a common goal. Ownership, control, and decision-making is distributed among all stakeholders, and they feel empowered to move forward with needed changes. In this model, as changes are made, data is collected at the beginning, the end, and at least once at a midpoint to prompt reflection on where things are going and how the library is getting there. The result is greater ownership of the changes and actions because of who is involved.

Summary

Personnel relationship assessments have added levels of complexity because they deal with colleagues and coworkers. The assessments have a stronger collaboration component and often ask employees to provide more information about their experiences and interactions and the associated emotions. For these reasons, increased sensitivity to individual privacy is needed. Consideration should be made to raise confidentiality to the level of anonymity during data collection, assessment, and dissemination. Doing so may require using outside evaluators and should always involve a review by the university's institutional review board.

The extra precautions and difficulties associated with conducting personnel relationship assessments does not make them easier, but it does make them better. The results can be used as a catalyst for increasing cooperation, collaboration, and improvement of all aspects of the library.

References

Cross, R., and Parker, A. (2004). *The hidden power of social networks: Understanding how work really gets done in organizations.* Harvard Business School Press.

Galbraith, Q., Merrill, E., and Outzen, O. (2018). The effect of gender and minority status on salary in private and public ARL libraries. *The Journal of Academic Librarianship, 44*(1), 75–80.

Silva, E., and Galbraith, Q. (2018). Salary negotiation patterns between women and men in academic libraries. *College and Research Libraries, 79*(3), 324–35.

Wilson, K. (2017). Collaborative leadership in public library service development. *Library Management, 39*(8/9), 518–29.

~

CHAPTER FOURTEEN

A Deep Bench

Staff Enrich Library Assessment Activities in an Academic Library

Joshua Tijerino, James Waters,
Kirsten Kinsley, Florida State University

This chapter discusses the professional development experiences of two library staff (nonfaculty librarians), Tijerino and Waters, as they changed the libraries' data management and visualization processes in two separate libraries on the campus of Florida State University (FSU), a Carnegie RU/HV (Research 1) institution. When the COVID-19 pandemic response forced many library employees to work remotely, there was an urgent need for comprehensive and timely data-gathering of remote library service activities. Tijerino and Waters, who grew professionally, discuss how they built trust and were empowered to fulfill new roles and responsibilities in the libraries as they improved the libraries' data management and visualization tools. The result benefited them personally and the libraries collectively as challenges and barriers were faced and overcome by listening to internal stakeholders, primarily faculty librarians and leaders.

Tijerino and Waters provided informed support and innovative datavisualization solutions to otherwise unidimensional and siloed public services datasets. Using Microsoft Teams, they met and cooperatively learned data management and visualization concepts and software to tell the story of library service and usage during the COVID-19 pandemic. These activities coalesced into an even larger employee-based group from other departments in the library to form the Assessment and Analytics Special Interest Group (SIG), which promotes assessment and analytics learning activities throughout the entire library organization. While changes to the data management and visualization are discussed in detail, this chapter draws attention to how library staff (nonfaculty librarians or library leadership) were supported and nurtured as they grew professionally and personally.

Literature Review

Library staff "are very critical to library service provision in academic libraries" (Ibegbulam and Eze, 2016, p. 483). Association of Research Libraries (ARL) Statistics for FSU Libraries shows that in the last twenty years the proportion of library staff compared to all library employees is trending downward from 52 percent of all library employees in 1999 to 29 percent of all library employees in 2019. This reality makes it even more critical for library staff to be well-trained and equipped to perform many diverse skill sets, including assessment and analytics skills.

A search for articles about library staff professional development to conduct assessment and analytics in libraries did not yield a lot of literature. Lakos and Phipps (2004) emphasized the importance of building a "culture of assessment" where the prerequisites involve library leadership committed to assessment and communicating its importance to library staff who ". . . recognize the value of it and engage in it as part of their regular assignments" (p. 353). A culture of assessment means that all library employees are engaged in assessment projects (ACRL, 2017, 11.3).

Zhang (2004) conducted a comprehensive study on library staffs' job-training needs and found that they are performing more and more faculty librarian duties and, therefore, should receive more training. His study included questions to library staff about their training needs. Those who responded indicated that they need more computer technology, interpersonal, supervisory, and management skills training.

While Zhang's study did not specifically mention assessment or analytics skills, data visualization and how to provide data in useful ways to library stakeholders is important. Data visualization is a highly technical skill that is challenging for both library staff and faculty librarians to learn. "Libraries must begin investing in their staff [all library employees] to help them develop these skills" (Chen, 2017, p. 26). Chen (2017) follows with:

In order to be able to employ data visualization, an institution must create opportunities for library staff [all library employees] to learn how to properly use this innovative, game-changing way of retrieving data. From there, a well-trained group of individuals in information visualization are better able to help those they serve. (p. 27)

Another challenge is learning how to present data in useful ways to stakeholders. Murphy (2013) states that ". . . the skills required to understand and analyze data differ significantly from the skills necessary to present data in a creative, compelling way" (p. 2). Both of those skills are needed. Fostering data exploration, both with the questions asked about it and how the story is shared, is essential in a thriving library culture assessment. The team collaboration and the corresponding staff experiences of Tijerino and Waters describe how FSU Libraries used professional development opportunities to help library staff develop solutions that circumvented COVID-19 restrictions and increased communication beyond the pandemic.

Team Collaboration

Stakeholder Solutions

Library staff, working in close collaboration with the assessment librarian and the senior applications analyst librarian, formed a Springshare Library Support Group (LSG). First, this group crowdsourced feedback through an open forum and survey of faculty librarians who use Springshare's LibInsight platform to record public service data transactions (i.e., reference and instruction) throughout the library. The LSG brainstormed with faculty librarians to determine ways that LibInsight datasets could better tell the story of what they do. Library staff understood that the LibInsight software could provide more than just transactional information for national survey requirements from library organizations such as the Association of College and Research Libraries and ARL. They worked to make data collection more streamlined and meaningful to faculty librarians and library leadership. The survey results also revealed that faculty librarians requested solutions about how to record asynchronous instruction and the development of digital learning tools. Since the library organization did not document this process anywhere in the organization, the LSG created a mock dataset to show how asynchronous instruction and digital learning tools could be recorded. Unfortunately, faculty librarians chose to not adopt the process. Instead, the LSG used an existing dataset to provide a short-term solution that was acceptable to faculty librarians. This scenario demonstrated that library staff could play an essential role in advocating solutions to data collection needs and be a catalyst for improvement.

Crowd-learning and Innovations in Data Visualization

Library staff innovated data analysis by creating data visualizations of the Lib-Insight dataset by importing it into Microsoft PowerBI (PBI) data visualization software. The LSG group crowd learned PBI together and demonstrated to faculty librarians the possibilities of using it to show a concise dashboard of the library's overall aggregate activities. They also created a mock individual faculty librarian's customized dashboard using PBI illustrating how it could be useful not just for a faculty librarian's professional evaluation documentation but could be leveraged to strategically plan future activities.

Tijerino and Waters were two library staff who were key to the entire process. They report on their personal experience of this process and how it encouraged them to be more involved in library interactions. They discuss the data collection and assessment of public service data and how crowd-learning and faculty librarian feedback continually shaped data visualizations.

Professional Development of Tijerino

Tijerino began in the library as a volunteer and a student worker before becoming a full-time nonlibrarian employee with the STEM Libraries Department after graduating with a bachelor's degree in biochemistry. He was first exposed to information science as a student worker but was willing to jump into the deep end and took on the steep learning curve. His role as a STEM Library associate involved many different support tasks, such as journal research, supporting instruction, or running events in partnership with registered student organizations on campus.

One of the first tasks assigned to him was to organize and maintain the statistics of the STEM Libraries. He familiarized himself with Springshare's LibInsight, including the nuances that allow efficient use with continuous utilization and practice. He developed a way of summarizing the librarian-patron interactions so that the STEM Libraries' employees could use those stats to help inform team-based decision-making. They looked at workshop attendance to determine which workshops to offer and developed future topics including the best times for subject librarian office hours. STEM Libraries' staff used the data to demonstrate the impact of reference consultations, instruction statistics, and other types of services. They examined trends to help understand what services and programs generate the most interest and engagement.

Tijerino observed that the LSG emphasized storytelling through statistics to support the whole library. This group was instrumental in his growth as an information professional. As a group, they began to learn new data visualization tools, such as PBI, in tandem with LibInsight datasets. The team discussed improving assessment tools so that stakeholders could glean the information from the data to make informed decisions.

In this group, Tijerino's colleagues guided him toward achieving his supervisor's goals to organize STEM libraries' departmental statistics, identified problems with data storytelling, and strove to improve them. His work was expedited by having a group of people who understood the data and who he could bounce ideas off and formulate concrete answers to questions posed by all library employees. Tijerino aided the group in solving data management issues, especially with cleaning up LibInsight data. Tijerino's interest in growing in his staff position led to many questions that this group helped him answer. It led to more meetings and increased interdepartmental relationships.

As a result of interactions with this group, professional trust developed with all STEM libraries' employees and beyond. There was an increase in confidence in library staff's ability to do their job. Tijerino felt less anxious when presenting to groups and analyzing data. He felt more prepared to serve all library employees and perform at the highest caliber. After working with the LSG, Tijerino formed the Assessment and Analytics SIG, under the Scholarly Support Network, a library-wide group dedicated to discussing important information science topics. The Assessment and Analytics SIG brought assessment-related problems and issues to a broader library stage. Tijerino's positive and optimistic attitude also helped break down barriers when interacting with anyone.

Professional Development of Waters

Waters faced two interconnected challenges. He needed to develop trust with faculty librarians and library staff by demonstrating his understanding and ability to use the PBI application while overcoming his self-doubt and becoming confident that he could do the job. These two challenges came together during an LSG meeting in early fall. He migrated summer public services data to PBI from Google sheets, including the number and type of interactions (reference or instruction) and format (e.g., email or chat). The library had severely scaled-back library services due to the COVID-19 pandemic and offered curbside delivery services. Faculty librarians and those running the new curbside service wanted to start gathering statistics of daily requests and departmental usage into a dataset.

Before the meeting, the LSG faced issues creating one PBI report that cleanly visualized data from multiple departments. To minimize data-management issues with a large dataset, the group divided the dataset up by STEM and main libraries, and then by departments. Each faculty librarian could create data visualizations based on the type of services provided (i.e., instruction, reference/research consultation), audience, and formats (e.g., emails, online chat, phone calls). This decision created a malleable foundation for displaying clean, consistent, and easily manageable reports for data visualization in PBI.

This decision allowed Waters to believe in his skill sets to analyze the data and remedied any issues faculty librarians felt concerning his capability to create data visualization. The PBI reports with smaller datasets focused on visualized information tailored to individual department activity and were a starting point for tangible storytelling on patrons' specific services. The team recognized that the curbside delivery report in PBI, with the area report option, was the best visualization for the curbside dataset as it allowed data visualization by academic department and items delivered (see figure 14.1). When the user hovered over the data area, a pop-up appeared and illustrated the amount of each item delivered and the type of item the library delivered to the selected academic department.

Everything came together at this meeting. Trust was built as the LSG pulled in the same direction. The collaborative environment fostered a digital workspace in which different approaches were tried. Through a cycle of feedback and revisions, the team came up with a viable solution. They tested the stacked area option and the line and clustered column chart. However, once they saw the area report and the pop-up with the details it provided, the team unanimously agreed that it worked best with the curbside report.

The curbside management teams' use of Waters' data visualization helped decide whether to expand the curbside service to more than one library or if the one pick-up location was enough. The data provided informed staffing decisions and prompted closer collaborations with faculty librarians whose departments were heavy users. Current discussions are ongoing whether this service might continue after COVID-19 protocols are relaxed and how services dovetail with the library delivery service that already exists (J. Hipsher, personal communication, December 10, 2020).

The benefit Waters experienced in this new role was a sense of empowerment. He is now invited to meetings with department heads more frequently.

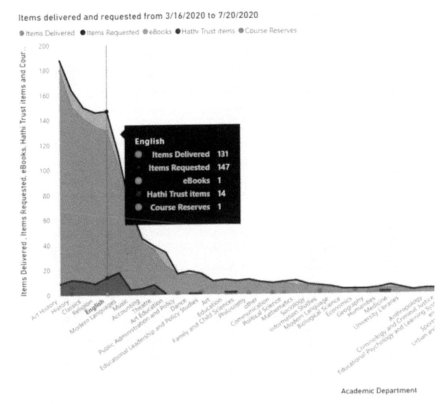

Items delivered and requested from 3/16/2020 to 7/20/2020

● Items Delivered ● Items Requested ● eBooks ● Hathi Trust Items ● Course Reserves

English

●	Items Delivered	131
	Items Requested	147
●	eBooks	1
	Hathi Trust items	14
●	Course Reserves	1

Academic Department

Figure 14.1.   Portion of the Curbside Delivery Visualization Using the PBI Area Report. Tijerino, Waters, Kinsley

He feels confident meeting with faculty librarians and library leadership with the excitement and drive to work with something useful for departments. Waters is motivated to understand what kind of data other library departments want and how they want it presented. For example, he contacted the Outreach Department and showed them a data visualization similar to the curbside report but one that visualized the event name, number of people who attended, and type of event. This visualization aided their decision-making. Waters also created a PBI report for the Access Services Department that provided a weekly rundown on their curbside data. This report prompted Access Services to request more data analytics and visualizations of their output to illustrate how much work library staff does. For them, data visualization became a useful tool for demonstrating departmental productivity.

Barriers, Challenges, and Benefits

Library Staff

Library staff wonder if faculty librarians will trust them to understand their data needs. Library staff assumed that their main hurdles would center on learning the PBI application and displaying a competency level. As it turned out, general communication issues were the most significant barrier. For example, library staff presented the work they did with LibInsight and PBI. They discussed the capability of PBI to migrate data from LibInsight and display stakeholder data in dashboards, which offered faculty librarians incredible data mobility and transparency. However, the conversation ended up focusing on a philosophical question of why data is collected. It was an incredibly beneficial opportunity for faculty librarians and library staff to collaborate and learn the PBI application together: to work alongside data professionals; to truly see and understand how they used data; and to learn applications offered library staff a visceral, professional development experience.

A great group of supportive colleagues with similar information science interests now discusses and answers questions that come up. It is invaluable to have people willing to help a colleague solve a problem that might have hindered an assigned task from being completed. It is also encouraging to watch others grow in confidence because there is a common interest shared in the group.

Library Benefits

This growing group of library staff and faculty librarians has given the Assessment Department a broader support system throughout the organization. Indeed, by involving library staff in this endeavor, assessment practices improved throughout the organization. Library staff can specifically address faculty librarian assessment and analytics inquiries to make those activities more informative and strategic. Simultaneously, library staff are empowered and equipped to perform those duties. Faculty librarians benefit because the library staff are in tune with and equipped to provide data needed to make decisions.

The newly formed Assessment and Analytics SIG became involved more broadly with assessment and analytics discussions and professional development activities. The group has since grown to include library staff from diverse departments in the libraries. "Developing a culture of assessment is about learning how to learn" (Lakos and Phipps, 2004, p. 359), and "it is built on trust. Trust can develop only in an environment where divergent positions can be articulated and differences discussed calmly and thoroughly—with an openness to incorporate new thinking" (Lakos and Phipps, 2004, p. 358). The newly formed Assessment and Analytics SIG will continue what Lakos and Phipps (2004) described above. Staff involvement in assessment and analytics is critical for a library-wide culture of assessment to prevail.

Next Steps

The SIG's purpose in the future, as stated in the FSU Libraries' internal wiki, is to:

> . . . to provide library faculty and staff with a forum to discuss topics and best practices for conducting assessment-related activities library-wide. This group will aim to be more inclusive of the broad range of assessment and programmatic evaluative needs and other related activities within the libraries. This group's primary mission is to advance and empower the assessment and program evaluation skills, abilities, and professional development of the entire organization. (December 2, 2020)

More specific projects include developing weekly dashboards of the public services dataset and training others to use PBI. The Assessment and Analytics SIG can determine what the professional development needs are for all library staff and faculty librarians.

Summary

A remote workforce during COVID-19 accelerated this collaborative process or even created the conditions for it to happen. Crowd-learning PBI screen-sharing using Microsoft Teams was very useful. In real time, the entire team could immediately see data presented in a variety of different chart formats. Data management issues that came up from data collection inconsistencies, and so on, could be detected immediately, and suggestions/troubleshooting made on the spot. If someone learned a tip or trick in PBI, they shared it with the group. Using a video-conferencing tool, such as Microsoft Teams or Zoom, with their screen-sharing features, facilitated hands-on learning as one participant can grant another member remote access to experiment or demonstrate solutions within the PBI platform.

Assessment data is de-siloed when all library employees come together to explore it and learn from each other about how to tell the data's story. Data visualizations can create meaning, and stories come alive with stakeholder dialogue. This Assessment and Analytics SIG approach helps build a culture of assessment for all libraries regardless if they have personnel dedicated to library assessment. Most importantly, faculty librarians and library staff learning crowd-learned data-visualization tools ask more fruitful questions and discover more innovative solutions when they work together. Library staff are the best conduit to the assessment librarian because they are the organization's eyes and ears as they serve on the frontlines. They often understand the data and workflow issues involved with data collection better than anyone in the organization. Empowering library staff boosts morale and fosters critical thinking skills, team building, and builds the skill set of library staff, which assists them for professional advancement.

Acknowledgment

Special acknowledgment for this chapter goes to Graduate Assistant Seol Lim and Senior Applications Analyst Librarian Matthew Burrell at FSU Libraries, who made significant contributions to the LSG Support Group and supported the writing of this chapter. The authors wish to dedicate this chapter to Matt, whose support of staff and encouragement was foundational in the success of this endeavor.

References

Association of College and Research Libraries (ACRL) Task Force on Standards for Proficiencies for Assessment Librarians and Coordinators. (2017, January 23). *ACRL proficiencies for assessment librarians and coordinators* (text). Association of College and Research Libraries (ACRL). http://www.ala.org/acrl/standards/assessment_proficiencies.

Chen, H. M. (2017). Information visualization. *Library Technology Reports*, 53(3), 1–30.

Ibegbulam, I., and Eze, J. U. (2016). Training needs of paraprofessional library staff in university libraries in South-East Nigeria. *Library Management; Bradford*, 37(8/9), 482–95.

Lakos, A., and Phipps, S. E. (2004). Creating a culture of assessment: A catalyst for organizational change. *Portal: Libraries and the Academy*, 4(3), 345–61. https://doi.org/10.1353/pla.2004.0052.

Murphy, S. A. (2013). Data visualization and rapid analytics: Applying Tableau desktop to support library decision-making. *Journal of Web Librarianship*, 7(4), 465–76. https://doi.org/10.1080/19322909.2013.825148.

Zhang, S. (2004). *A study of the job training needs of the support staff in the six Kansas Board of Regents University Libraries* [dissertation]. Kansas State University. https://krex.k-state.edu/dspace/bitstream/handle/2097/46/ShaliZhang2005.pdf?sequence=1&isAllowed=y.

~

CHAPTER FIFTEEN

Sorting Out Library Programs, Services, and Tasks

Identifying Strategic Connections

Kelley Martin and Cindy Thompson,
University of Missouri-Kansas City

Introduction

This story discusses organizing and documenting information about a library's work, which developed into a story about building a culture of trust and understanding between siloed departments. Over the previous decade, the libraries have engaged in multiple reorganizations, mostly focused on administrative decision-making, to address staffing changes, budget shortfalls, and shifts in priorities. The most recent restructuring at the University of Missouri–Kansas City (UMKC) was the result of severe budget reductions and several layoffs. Employees were exhausted and demoralized, as each change resulted in unexpected consequences. Library leadership knew that ongoing reactive reorganization was not an option and they needed to position the organization to better support employees' long-term reality—budgets, service needs, and staffing models that would change. The libraries' administration resolved to undertake a holistic restructuring that would include all individuals and aspects of the libraries. The critical aspect of that process was a comprehensive assessment of structure and environment.

In any project involving research and assessment of an organization, broad involvement and input opportunities are critical for success. Thus, the Project Management Team (PMT) had outcomes that focused on collaboration and building a shared culture of understanding that intended to:

- create a definitive list of library services that map to library programs;
- develop a shared language around programs, services, and tasks;
- build consensus for core library services and inform the prioritization of those services; and
- encourage an understanding of the interconnectedness of library work.

To achieve these outcomes, library employees engaged in a highly collaborative process, starting with the most detailed level of work, categorizing these items into higher-level services and programs, and then breaking the list back down into tasks and subtasks. Thus far, employees divided the work into two distinct phases—one in which high-level programs and services were identified, and a second in which connections to tasks and subtasks were made.

One component of this process was the makeup of the PMT. The initial review of existing literature revealed that no process appeared to meet the libraries' needs. Instead, the PMT decided to draw upon their expertise and experience to design a process that would achieve the desired outcomes. The PMT's unique makeup and individual expertise allowed adaption and planning as the project progressed, which supported the collaborative aspects of this work because employees were all learning together. The PMT had three members:

Vicki Kirby, library information specialist senior media cataloger, who has a strong eye for detail and a fresh perspective on both the libraries' and the project's methodologies. She is a member of the libraries' staff.

Kelley Martin, assessment and user research coordinator, who has a strong background in qualitative methodologies, usability testing, and needs-assessment. She is a member of the libraries' faculty.

Cindy Thompson, interim dean, who has a strong background in quantitative methodologies, organizational structures, and organizational change. She is an administrator for the libraries.

We also consulted with others in the libraries when specific needs or a different perspective was required. Together, a general process for the three major parts of the assessment was developed focusing on program and service identification, task and subtask mapping, and capacity analysis (see table 15.1). For the purposes of this chapter, the following definitions are provided.

- Program: General area of responsibility/work in the libraries in support of the libraries' mission.

Table 15.1. Activities Within the Three-Part Process

Program and Service Identification	Task and Subtask Mapping	Capacity Analysis
Departmental work inventories	Task inventory	Departmental focus groups
Card sort activity	Mapping tasks to services, services to programs, tasks to departments	Documentation of workflows
Focus groups		Troubleshooting problems
Card sort activity		Identification of capacity opportunities and needs
Open feedback period		

- Service: Specific area of responsibility/work in the libraries in support of a program.
- Task: Specific work completed in the libraries in support of a service.
- Subtask: Specific tasks that require individual expertise.

Methodology

Program and Service Identification

The PMT's first job, developing a definitive list of library services and programs, began with a task familiar to website usability testers—a card sort (Neilson, 2004). To begin this phase, every library department or team created work inventories, a process led by department heads with PMT member assistance. To provide a framework for the inventory, department heads were instructed to include anything complex enough that one might consider writing documentation to complete the work.

Each item listed on the inventory was printed on cards, which the department was asked to complete together during a focus group. The cards included a form asking:

- the outcome of the activity,
- whether the activity was a program, service, or task,
- primary department that performs the activity,
- other departments involved, and
- priority (ranked one through four, with four being a high priority).

To provide a frame of reference and to build a common language, the definitions of key terms above were shared with each group, and participants were instructed to consider the libraries' mission as they made their decisions in completing the forms. This part of the activity took about one hour.

For the second hour, departments sorted the tasks into specific services, assigned each service to a library program, and created new cards for unlisted programs and services. While the participants were filling and sorting cards, the PMT listened to conversations and noted discussions and insights. This "listening" information was invaluable in future phases as team members worked to reconcile the card sorts into a single dataset.

Once the services were combined this into a dataset, the PMT worked toward defining programs. Because the PMT was present for all card sorts and discussions, they formed a test focus group and went through the program cards to develop a draft of consolidated and sorted programs. Then two small focus groups from the faculty governance group and the staff advocacy group were formed to review the programs identified by all combined departmental card sorts. Participants only considered services as a part of this phase in clarifying a program. While the two teams resorted cards, members of the PMT again listened to conversations and noted discussions and insights during the participants' decision-making process.

The three card sorts produced similar results but with very different language. Team members used Tableau to create grouped variables, pulling together services under each identified program. This exercise allowed the PMT to see where each group put each service and to consolidate where there was as much agreement as possible.

At this point, the PMT invited feedback in checking its work. A major barrier throughout this activity was language. For example, "access" can describe cataloging and metadata, circulation, website, and physical space. PMT members commonly heard "we can't call it X, because that would also include Y, which we put in Z." For this reason, descriptive language was used rather than attempting to name programs when sharing, allowing employees to focus on the idea rather than the terminology.

While awaiting feedback, PMT members started work on services. At this point, it became necessary to separate services from their identified programs and conduct an abbreviated version of the initial analysis. PMT members relabeled activities as services, subservices, and tasks, before reassigning them to programs.

Using the data from the previous step, PMT members printed new service cards that listed:

- new activity type,
- adjusted activity name,
- subservice name (when applicable),
- program name,

- original activity name,
- original department listing that service, and
- original priority ranking.

The volume of services was such that the three core PMT members, who continued to attend all sessions, conducted an initial sort. They grouped similar services with generic (not departmental) terminology, defined more activities as tasks, and tweaked programs based on included services. They also introduced new terminology to address ideas that were often sticking points. These definitions included:

- Tasks: services that support programs, which support the libraries' mission.
- Initiatives: big picture strategic investments, not yet structurally established but supportive of the libraries' mission.
- Projects: things done with an end date that require investment from services and tasks.
- Tools: things used (nouns) that are often critical and require many services to maintain.

The PMT members introduced the resultant hierarchy of programs and services to administration and department heads for member checking and outcomes assignment, who adjusted based on the feedback. Finally, department heads and library leadership took the sorted cards and made additional connections between departments before sharing a report to all library employees for review.

Task and Subtask Mapping

Shortly after completion of the Program and Service Review, the libraries' Restructuring Coordinating Task Force determined that the libraries needed to complete an analysis of individual and departmental workloads. The PMT decided to build on the completed work and began with mapping tasks and departments to those carefully defined programs and services.

First, the PMT members revisited the initial step, the work inventory. Using the new standard definitions, they pulled work from previous levels of analysis to draft a preliminary list of all libraries' tasks. They then used a semi-structured interview process to check these lists with departments, adding new tasks and removing others. In consultation with departments, they combined tasks that crossed departments and distinguished those that required specialized training. The PMT then removed duplicates, assigned departments to tasks, and mapped them to programs and services. The result of this review was a complete map of programs, services, tasks, and departments, which provides a comprehensive view of the libraries' work (see figure 15.1).

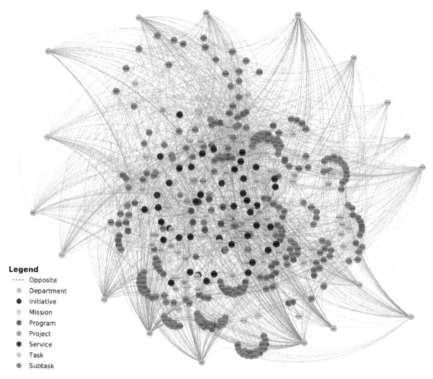

Legend
- - - - Opposite
- ◉ Department
- ● Initiative
- ◎ Mission
- ● Program
- ◉ Project
- ● Service
- ◉ Task
- ● Subtask

Figure 15.1. Comprehensive Map of Programs, Services, Tasks, Departments, and Other Activities. Martin, Thompson

Capacity Analysis

While working through the task and subtask mapping, the PMT members simultaneously began the work of the capacity analysis. Again, no existing process was identified that truly achieved the libraries' goal of understanding and identifying gaps and opportunities in capacity, so the PMT members developed their own process. They began as before by talking with all library employees. Prior to scheduling meetings with departments, they asked all employees to complete a reflective personal self-assessment. Each individual completed this brief exercise with no expectation of sharing, since the purpose of the exercise was to help everyone start thinking and reflecting on the good and bad of their work in preparation for departmental meetings. However, department heads were encouraged to share personal examples from this process during the group sessions to help promote open and honest communication.

Next, the PMT members sent preliminary simple task lists from the task and subtask inventory to each department to use as a reference point during discussions. In these interviews, employees attempted to tease out problems, opportunities, and needs. The intention was to end each meeting with an initial proposal from the PMT with tools to meet departmental needs. However, the PMT members learned after the first of these meetings that the issues to address within a single department were minimal and largely supervisory. The majority of issues and opportunities were systemic and required that they address them on a larger scale. Thus, they waited until all interviews were complete before beginning action plans. Unfortunately, the work of developing these plans and identifying opportunities for systemic change coincided with COVID-19 and will resume when able.

Results

This process initially focused on gathering information for a restructuring, though there were additional goals of communicating interconnectedness and establishing a shared vocabulary. In the end, employees learned far more than needed for restructuring. They achieved the outcomes and more, developing a foundation for a more open and connected library and identifying a broad range of applications for the results throughout the libraries. As a member of the PMT, an administrator was able to use the information learned through all steps of this process in information, advocacy, decision-making, and planning—particularly when she was appointed interim dean late in the project.

The work was foundational in providing a structure for establishing and mapping priorities for adjustment in the short-term and for investment opportunities in the long term. The libraries' Dean's Leadership Group (DLG) used the initial programs and services review as a comprehensive view of the ways the libraries supported the university's mission. Administration mapped the programs and service to strategy—either as top-level strategic plan goals or as key initiatives required by our campus, our university system, or that existed in several areas of the strategic plan. The DLG then ranked the list according to priorities, established exactly what additional support was needed, and determined how to provide that support. This process drove much of the reorganization.

For example, one of the identified services was "Create and Maintain Access for Electronic Resources" under the general program of "Collections." This service mapped to the strategic plan's goal III: assure collections meet the needs of UMKC academic programs and research. Through the process, DLG determined that it was a high-priority need, identified that staff time was not clearly dedicated to this area and that it was not receiving sufficient support, and established an action in order to address the problem. In this example, administration addressed the needs partly through the reorganization and partly through workflow analysis. Other instances of identified priorities resulted in successful arguments made to the provost for strategic hiring funding, reallocating internal funding to focus on priorities, and changes to fundraising strategies.

Additional results achieved throughout the process were a deep understanding of the libraries and of the work each department does, which has increased the understanding of the interconnectedness of what libraries do on a daily basis. Employees consistently found that work done in disparate library departments was strongly interconnected. For example, reference work cannot be accomplished without the cataloging or collections departments. This outcome might seem obvious, but somehow in the daily course of an employee's work, the nonpublic service type work does not tend to get the glory and public accolades that those in front-facing departments receive. Without the behind-the-scenes work, a library would not function. This outcome was evident throughout participant conversations, starting with initial card sorts. However, nothing illustrated it as well as the final analysis, which mapped individual tasks to departments. The number of departments that shared work and the number of services any department touched was astounding. Even though these findings resulted in a visualization that was difficult to read, that alone was telling. Any staff attrition through retirement or resignation could be analyzed clearly and readily with this information.

A less positive but still beneficial outcome of this work became apparent when the university began facing more dramatic budget constraints than usual. First, strategic funding vanished in late 2019, and more when the COVID-19 pandemic struck in 2020. Revisiting priorities allowed library leadership to ensure that they were mindful in decision-making in a time of crisis. Long term, this information also supports discussion of the far-reaching impact of budget reductions on a library. Having a clear, concise summary of the libraries' programs (and their connected services) helps to communicate with the campus and university leadership when questions arise about further reductions. At UMKC, additional budget reductions may result in recommendations to cut or merge full programs. This project allows libraries' leadership to easily demonstrate the impact of those reductions through being able to identify how that work is connected to other areas and what specifically is related to that program.

Summary and Next Steps

Throughout this endeavor, several things became critically clear for this process and future assessments. While it is often the instinct of library workers to document things—often to a far greater extent than necessary—there can be added benefits if librarians are willing to pay as much attention to the process as to the result. Listening, documenting, and developing a shared understanding is good for everyone, as it creates empathy and appreciation for others' work. The addition of shared vocabulary is also beneficial. In many sessions, individuals who seemed to disagree with each other initially found out that they were simply using different terms to describe the same thing. Intentional questioning and careful defining helped resolve a number of conflicts within the process, when workflow analysis began, and during the assignment of work.

Participation in this process was also greatly beneficial to the PMT members, who were able to grow in their understanding of the general work the libraries accomplished and the very detailed processes that individual employees accomplished. The process helped the assessment and user research coordinator build better relationships with all library workers, as well as a deeper understanding of library work, which translates to better assessment project planning. The interim dean was able to understand the areas that were new to her oversight on a much deeper level.

Unfortunately, the COVID-19 pandemic slowed the work. There is still a need for more cross-checking with departments to ensure that the mapping is accurate, and some documents—especially the priorities—require updating. The team was unable to finish the capacity analysis, so there is still a need to analyze job descriptions and develop customized action plans for individual departments as well as a general plan for systemic changes in the libraries. Some adjustments were made based on lessons learned, primarily in communications and in provision of centralized support, but the team and DLG have yet to fully analyze the findings thus far.

Finally, a key finding is that the process of interviewing all departments and including all individuals in the organization in conversation is a good time investment for everyone. Thus, the PMT members hope to continue this work over time for the purpose of both updating the documentation as well as continuing to understand each other more fully.

References

Neilson, J. (2004, July 18). *Card sorting: How many users to test.* Nielson Norman Group. https://www.nngroup.com/articles/card-sorting-how-many-users-to-test/.

~

CHAPTER SIXTEEN

Communication Networks Within an Academic Library

Holt Zaugg

Communication networks are used by organizations to better understand how people within the organization interact with one another (Moolenaar, 2012; Sparrowe et al., 2001). The communication patterns inform connections among employees that describe how information does or may flow to enhance innovation and productivity (Tsai and Ghoshal, 1998). Other communication network studies focus on how communication patterns change when organizational structures change (Liben-Nowell and Kleinberg, 2007), differences among an organization's departments or between organizations (Nicolaou and Birley, 2003), and communication factors that affect employees' decision-making abilities (Blau and Alba, 1982).

Bavelas (1950) described four patterns of information flow between people. The first pattern is linear (A to B to C), in which employees communicate through adjacent coworkers in a linear fashion, hindering direct communication between nonadjacent individuals. The second and third patterns restrict access to a group of employees or to a leader through a single individual. The fourth pattern gives employees unfettered access to each other, creating open communication and information-sharing. While this open pattern is often touted as the best pattern, there are specific cases for which the other patterns are appropriate.

Moolenaar (2012) recommended using multiple levels of communication analysis to determine the communication efficacy among employees. Hanneman and Riddle (2005) supported this position of examining the connectedness of employees to utilize their expertise and experience as they create innovative solutions that will solve or prevent problems. However, identifying communication patterns is complicated, especially when considering group size, communication modalities (e.g., email, phone calls, face-to-face), and communication levels and directionality.

This study examines the employee communication patterns within the Harold B. Lee Library (Lee Library) by identifying communication patterns between employees. The model allows librarians to identify their level of communication with all other library employees using all communication modalities.

Description of the Lee Library

At the time of this assessment, the Lee Library had approximately 160 employees working in one of six divisions: administration, administrative services, library information technology (LIT), public services, special collections, and technical services. Each division had multiple departments and varied in the number of employees depending on duties. Employees work on one of six floors in an area equivalent to eleven football fields.

Method

Several factors were considered to address this assessment's complexity. A pilot with one library division (LIT) was used to help identify and clarify design features prior to conducting the study with the entire library. Several key aspects of the assessment were considered. These include identifying all of the potential levels of communication. Using Hanneman and Riddle (2005) and Moolenaar (2012), we identified and created six levels of communication:

A = No communication or interaction
B = As Needed: An immediate or short-term interaction
C = Minimal: Simple communication, such as a monthly newsletter
D = Moderate: Medium amount of interaction
E = Strong: Recurring important interaction
F = Deep: Frequent, intense, and complex interactions

Given the advancement in communications and the roles some employees have with specific communications (e.g., social media specialist), the potential modalities of communication were identified but not differentiated. Employees were asked to consider face-to-face, email, telephone calls, and texting communications with other employees, but communications via social media platforms were excluded. The communication was also limited to work-related issues, eliminating personal communications between friends. While employees were asked to consider each of these types of communication modalities, no attempt was made to differentiate between the modalities as the communication between employees was more important than the modality used for communicating. This decision significantly reduced the complexity of responses for employees and the analysis of data.

Considering Bernard et al.'s (1984) examination of several case studies that indicated people had difficulty recalling or predicting communications with others, it was felt that a sufficient but limited timeframe was needed in view of some of the types of employee interactions, for example, instances where employees worked with each other on a project for a few months with strong or deep communications but had minimal or no communication prior to or following the project. For this reason, a timeframe of communications over the past year was used, knowing that there would be gaps and that employee perceptions of communication would not necessarily match their actual communications. Considerations for data collection and analysis were also part of the design phase but are discussed in the following sections.

Since employees had to indicate their level of communication with all other employees, a survey was used over a three-week period to collect data. Employees could stop and return to the survey several times if needed. Library and division leadership supported the assessment by providing time for a library-wide presentation on the assessment followed by questions from employees. They also encouraged employees within their respective divisions to participate in the survey and allowed surveys to be completed on the clock.

Using Hanneman and Riddle (2005) and Moolenaar (2012), protocols on how best to analyze and disseminate the data were determined. First, the data was organized so visual, interactive communication webs could be created for each division at each communication level. Geometric symbols were used to identify library divisions, and colors were used to identify departments within a division (color is not shown in the web example; see figure 16.1). The first two letters of the first and last names of each employee were used to identify individuals (for example, "JaDo" for "Jane Doe") to help simplify the figure. Second, the concept of a communication unit (CU) was created, which is defined as a single, one-way communication between two people regardless of modality used or communication level. For example, a communication from Joyce to Ted would be considered one CU, and a communication from Ted to Joyce would be considered a second CU. Tables were made according to Haythornthwaite's (1996) five categories using CUs to better understand communication patterns, with the exception that the range category was replaced with an obscurity category. Category descriptions are provided in the findings section.

Network Webs

Network webs are visual representations of communications between library employees. Using a special add-on to Excel, interactive webs allow employees to see where communication networks are strong, where they are weak, and who is isolated at each communication level.

When possible, colors and symbols are used to provide a clear picture of where communication is working and where it is not. Figure 16.1 indicates several positive and negative communication pathways at the deep com-

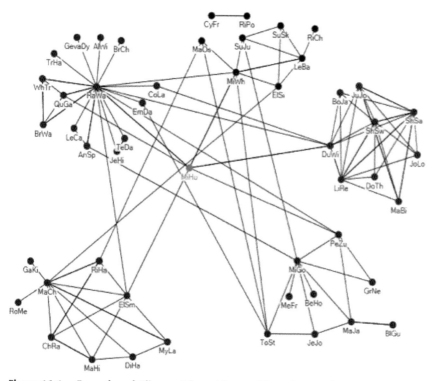

Figure 16.1. Examples of Cliques, Obscurities, and Prominences in a Division at the Deep Level. Zaugg

munication level. On the middle right, the group is well-connected, with multiple communication pathways within the group. However, losing DuWi would cut this group off from communications from all other groups. At the top, CyFr and RiPo are completely isolated from all others. Communication patterns vary depending on the communication levels. Examining the network web enables employees to determine where bottlenecks or isolation occur and need to be addressed.

No attempt was made to determine significant differences between departments, divisions, or employees as the purpose of the assessment was to identify communication patterns within the Lee Library. Knowing the patterns would help employees continue with these communication patterns or make changes. No one type of communication pattern is better or worse than another, but each serves its purpose given the employee's current tasks and responsibilities. The analysis only captured communication patterns at a moment in time.

Findings

Results for this assessment were presented to all employees in an oral presentation, a summary report, and, where requested, personal communication reports. The presentation included instructions on how to use an interactive network web to examine different levels of communication with other employees. A brief synopsis of the assessment's results is provided in the following paragraph.

Moolenaar (2012) suggested that an 80 percent response rate is needed to reach a threshold to determine reliable patterns. The threshold was only reached by two of the library divisions, with another three divisions coming within 7 percent of this threshold and one division falling far below the threshold (65 percent), with an overall response rate of 75 percent. As this was the first attempt to identify communication patterns, these rates were considered sufficient. Hereafter, results are discussed by category.

Cohesion
Cohesion describes the amount and types of relationships among division employees, disaggregated by each division and, where appropriate, departments. The total percent of CUs at each communication level for each department within each division was examined. For most departments, communication largely occurred at the moderate, strong, or deep levels, indicating strong communication patterns within departments. Communication patterns within the Social Sciences, Learning Commons, Special

Collections, and Cataloging and Metadata Departments indicated minimal or as needed communication patterns. These patterns may relate to the nature of work done by specific employees that only requires minimal communication. Of concern is the high percentage of no communication contact among employees within the Cataloging and Metadata and Materials Acquisitions Departments. These results indicate isolated employees and a need to examine communication patterns among them.

Similar comparisons were made between each division at each communication level indicating the strongest communication patterns used. For example, administration's strongest communication pattern with other divisions is as-needed, indicating that communication occurs only when there is a need to communicate. In communications between all other divisions, the most dominant pattern is no communication. This pattern indicates a hierarchal structure where most of the rank-and-file do not directly communicate with other library employees but receive communications from library leadership through division and department leaders. If a flatter communication structure is desired, communication changes would need to be made to these patterns.

Structural Equivalence

Structural equivalence identifies if the directionality of the communications is happening at the same level between any two employees. Communication levels do not need to be the same between employees because the information being communicated may differ for the two employees, but ideally, they should be somewhat similar. For example, Joyce indicates communication with Ted at an as-needed level, but Ted indicates communications with Joyce at a minimal level. Ted may send out a monthly newsletter to the library regarding his duties, but Joyce only communicates with Ted if she has a specific question arising from the newsletter.

At the divisional level, the communication directionality helps library employees and leadership understand if the flow of information should be more identical or if there are specific reasons for the directionality. On an individual level an employee can evaluate outgoing and incoming communications to determine if there is a justified reason for the difference (e.g., information newsletters) or if the communication level between individuals needs to be adjusted.

Prominence

Prominence measures the potential communication networks available between employees and the percentage that is used. Obviously, direct communication would be best, but if direct communication is not possible, information may be sent through an intermediary through another communication pathway. No employee uses every possible pathway but having communication network options ensures additional pathways are available to use. Matrix multiplication provides a means to determine the total number of pathways between employees in an organization. Only at the no-contact level is a pathway blocked and prominence diminished.

Prominence among library divisions in the Lee Library ranged from a high of 100% for Administrative Services to a low of 48% for Technical Services. The fewer employees a division had, the more likely all communication pathways were used, indicating a free flow of information. Lower percentages may be an indication of a hierarchal communication structure.

Obscurity

Obscurity is the percentage of employees reporting the no-contact level between divisions and departments. This hinders communication since employees do not send or receive information. In extreme cases, employees have no connections to others or only one connection.

Obscurity in the Lee Library ranged from a low of 0 percent for Administrative Services to a high of 32 percent for Technical Services. In all instances, rates of obscurity should be closely examined to determine if any employee is isolated from others, either physically (e.g., employees working on different floors) or in some other way.

Brokerage

Brokerage is the most common communication level used within and between divisions. Within the Lee Library, no contact is the most common level used between all divisions, with Administration being the exception as communication occurs at the as-needed level.

Value and Decision-Making

Organizationally, a communication network assists the library employees in making connections with other employees and eliminating bottlenecks to facilitate problem-solving and innovation. Such a change may require a flattening of a communication network. For example, a previous leader of all library IT employees required any requests for work be made through him. After he departed, the new leader allowed any library employee to contact any library IT employee. This hierarchical flattening increased the flow of information. Problems were solved more quickly, and innovations became more common.

On a personal level, library employees can examine their interactions with other employees and adjust the level of communication accordingly. While adjustments require the cooperation of both employees, the network analysis allows the employee and their supervisor to know where such communications may improve library employee interactions and the resulting benefits to patrons.

Summary

A communication network analysis enables library employees to see where and how communication occurs and at what levels. The degree of communication allows employees to determine whether they have the proper amount of interaction or if adjustments need to be made so employees are not isolated or become communication bottlenecks. The resulting increased communication allows information to flow more freely within the library, improving problem-solving and innovation.

References

Bavelas, Alex. (1950). Communication patterns in task-oriented groups. *The Journal of the Acoustical Society of America*, 22(6), 725–30.

Bernard, H., Killworth, P., Kronenfeld, D., and Sailor, L. (1984). The problem of important accuracy: The validity of retrospective data. *Annual Review Anthropology*, 13, 495–517.

Blau, J. R., and Alba, R. D. (1982). Empowering nets of participation. *Administrative Science Quarterly*, 27(3), 363–79.

Hanneman, R., and Riddle, M. (2005). *Introduction to social network methods* (volume thirteen). University of California Press.

Haythornthwaite, C. (1996). Social network analysis: An approach and technique for the study of information exchange. *Library Information Science Research*, 18(4), 323–42.

Liben-Nowell, D., and Kleinberg, J. (2007). The link-prediction problem for social networks. *Journal of the American Society for Information Science and Technology*, 58(7), 1019–31.

Moolenaar, N. (2012). A social network perspective on teacher collaboration in schools: Theory, methodology and applications. *American Journal of Education*, 119(1), 7–39.

Nicolaou, N., and Birley, S. (2003). Social networks in organizational emergence: The university spinout phenomenon. *Management Science*, 49(12), 1702–25.

Sparrowe, R., Liden, R., Wayne, S., and Kraimer, M. (2001). Social networks and the performance of individuals and groups. *The Academy of Management Journal,* 44(2), 316–25.

Tsai, W., and Ghoshal, S. (1998). Social capital and value creation: The role of intrafirm networks. *The Academy of Management Journal,* 41(4), 464–76.

⌒

CHAPTER SEVENTEEN

What's Next?

Holt Zaugg

A colleague and mentor always asked, "So what?" at the end of any research presentation as a means to help researchers see beyond their findings and identify their importance in the world. In this chapter his phrase is modified to "What's next?" in an attempt to extend thinking beyond what has been discussed in this book. The end of this book should really be the beginning of assessing better. Everyone is at a different place in their assessment program. Some may already be doing some of the things discussed in this chapter, but by examining the current state of your library assessments and looking back, you are able to gain a vision of where to go next and how those assessments may inform a future vision of the library.

In an article regarding the future of libraries, Miguel Figueroa (2018) outlined several guiding principles to help envision the future of libraries. His ideas included:

- witnessing trends and patterns
- examining the ways students learn and behave
- experiencing what happens in classrooms, instruction, and other areas of the library
- noticing what and how things are changing

Daily focused observations using these principles and understanding the way they interact with each other helps library employees see things differently. Instead of marching forward with a daily "to-do" list, they begin to see a future for the library and how their daily actions contribute to that future. Much like symbiotic organisms that depend on each other, library employees begin to see how daily library interactions, assessments, and a future vision fit together and inform one another. These symbiotic relationships facilitate the examination of trends, patterns, and changes that expand the vision of future opportunities for the library and how to achieve a future vision.

Using the assessment tasks outlined in chapter 1, this chapter discusses how potential changes to each assessment task can influence assessment. The temptation is to see changes as unique to each assessment task, but the symbiotic relationships among assessment tasks means that changes to one task may influence other tasks. For example, the types of data collection decided upon in the design task affect how that data is analyzed or disseminated. The following changes discussed for each assessment task will often "bleed" over into other tasks. Additionally, these changes are not the only potential changes to assessment tasks. As a library employee reads about and engages in assessments, their eyes will be opened to how things may be done better.

Design

As a culture of assessment develops within a library, the design of assessments will adjust. One change focuses on the iterative nature of assessments and when assessments should be repeated. Additionally, innovative approaches will need to be taken to mitigate the effects of strained budgets and limited resources. This section describes three potential changes.

Iteration

Assessments are either formative or summative. Summative assessments examine a change after it is completed to determine if the change was just something different or, in fact, something better. Formative assessments are ongoing and enable frequent adjustments to how things are done. Both types of assessment work together to inform change. For example, when the Lee Library wanted to change the individual study desks (ISDs) from a box-on-stilts shape to one that better fit students' current study needs, formative and summative assessments were used. The formative assessments began with asking students what changes they wanted. This data was used by a creativity bootcamp class to design new ISDs. Two prototype ISDs were built, assessed, adjusted, and redesigned to make the final ISD. These formative assessments informed step-by-step changes to the ISDs. After about half of the old ISDs were replaced with the new ISDs, a summative assessment was conducted to determine if the new ISDs were working as intended and functioning better than the old ISDs (Zaugg and Belliston, 2020).

The timeframe for repeating assessments depends on several factors, including what is being assessed, who uses what is being assessed, and the type of institution the library is supporting. To illustrate, if a library released a new website, it should conduct a summative assessment of the website to determine how well the website functions and to create a baseline for future assessments. If the institution is a two-year college, a repeated website assessment should occur in two or three years. If the institution is a four-year college, the assessment should be repeated in four to five years. The time span ensures that a new population of students is part of the website assessment.

Hogan and Hutson (2018) proposed an iterative five-step assessment cycle to improve library services. The time taken to implement all five steps (data collection, data analysis, plan improvement, data sharing and planning, and implementation) varies depending on the project, but the intent is to repeat the plan every five years. Doing so enables the library to reexamine the services and reflect on the impact of changes while looking forward to what additional changes are needed.

As a library develops a culture of assessment, both summative and formative assessments gain prominence in library decision-making. Each time an assessment occurs, questions should be asked to determine whether the assessment should be summative (one-and-done) or if formative assessments need to occur, and, if so, when the assessments should occur. Answering these questions allows the library to plan for future assessments so some aspect of the library is assessed, changed, and forgotten or worse not assessed at all (Zaugg, 2018).

Resource Support

Two types of support are critical to assessments. The first is financial. This support includes the salaries for full- and part-time nonstudent library employees and for part-time student employees, as well as money for equipment (e.g., computers, video cameras, analysis applications). These costs are typically built into library budgets. If budgets are tight, employees conducting assessments may arrange to borrow some equipment from resources the library lends out (e.g., borrowing a video camera to conduct an assessment instead of buying one).

The other support is logistical. This support enlists the help of library employees and others outside of the library. If a library is examining the incidence of browsing in their stacks, they may enlist employees who work at the reference desk or reshelve items or library security to count the number of people browsing the library stacks as they perform their jobs. Using others takes time to coordinate, but it leads to greater participation in and ownership of library assessments.

Logistical support from outside the library includes training on how to use data collection and analysis tools and collaborations between library assessment and faculty teaching qualitative or quantitative analysis classes in several university departments (e.g., sociology, psychology, or educational research). These collaborations serve several purposes that create multiple win-win situations (Zaugg and Child, 2016). First, the library is able to conduct assessments that require multiple in-person hours to collect and analyze the data. Second, faculty teaching these courses often experience a positive change in their relationships with their students as they often switch roles from a "sage on the stage" to someone working in the trenches with students. They become coresearchers with students as they solve issues and problems occurring in the assessment. Third, students have a learning experience that helps them apply theoretical learning in a real-world situation. If the class ends with students presenting their findings to library leadership, the assessment becomes a complete package for the students to use on their CVs or in future job interviews. Fifth, when results are presented to library leadership, the perspective is through the eyes of students. Library leadership can ask questions of students during a presentation of findings to better understand students' perspectives.

Prototyping

Prototyping originates in product design and development, but it is being used more in educational settings. It focuses on taking small, incremental steps in a library project with repeated formative assessments as an integral part of the prototype to determine the project is moving in the correct direction (Zaugg et al., 2020). By combining small design and development decisions with assessment, library employees are able to stop a process before it becomes a boondoggle or make incremental adjustments to achieve a goal that is cost-effective, useful, and wanted.

Data Collection

Those involved in research have their preferred data collection and analysis tools. However, if these tools are the only ones used, data collection and analysis become limited. As the saying goes, "If the only tool you have is a hammer, everything looks like a nail!" It is necessary to continue to learn about and try out new data collection tools to ensure that different perspectives and groups are given a voice in each assessment. The impact of only two of many aspects of data collection are discussed.

Triangulation

Triangulation refers to using different data collection tools in an assessment to collect different types of data that support or refute collected data. Triangulation becomes increasingly important as the library moves to a culture of assessment.

Contradictory data from different collection methods indicates a need for more data to be collected and examined to explain the contradictions. Triangulation may occur by changing the assessment tool or the person collecting the data. For example, Washburn and Bibb (2011) emphasized the importance of training undergraduate students to collect data from fellow undergraduates for library assessments. This process allows undergraduate students who participate in the assessment to speak freely and be more forthcoming with a peer rather than trying to supply answers they think a library evaluator wants. The essence of triangulation is having the right tools administered by the right people.

If collected data from different tools tell the same story, the additional data help to substantiate decisions that need to be made. As library employees expand the repertoire of assessment tools, they can pick and choose tools that best fit the assessment and help them to better understand what is happening.

Balance

While identification of all affected groups takes place in the design assessment task, implementation ensuring that all stakeholder groups are asked to participate in the assessment occurs in the data collection task. Balance includes groups from a variety of demographic identifiers (e.g., gender, race, socioeconomic status). All groups associated with the assessment need to be represented in appropriate ways during the assessment. For example, if your library has rooms dedicated for faculty to use for scholarship activities, the assessment involves only faculty, and no students would be asked to participate. However, all faculty (e.g., without and with tenure and at all rank levels) should be asked to participate. Additionally, faculty who are currently using these spaces, those who have used the spaces but are no longer using them, and those who have never used the spaces should be invited to participate to ensure that the perspectives of each group are heard and understood.

Data Analysis

Data analysis will continue to follow the prescribed methods for both quantitative and qualitative data, and these methods will evolve as new developments and procedures are refined. One recent development is the use of data analytics in understanding student-use patterns. While data analytics are used in business to understand shoppers' buying patterns, it has been used less by education and libraries because of privacy issues. However, data analytics, especially in partnership with university-level analysts, helps identify students with academic needs so that actions can be taken to help them before they drop out of university. Additionally, data analytics identifies where and how collections need to grow by examining use patterns so resources are spent wisely. Precautions need to be taken to preserve patron privacy, but data analytics are is here to help.

Litsey and Mauldin (2018) discussed how they used predictive analytics and machine learning to improve products and services for library patrons. Their system (called Automated Library Information Exchange Network, or ALIEN) helped library employees understand the movement of items in the library via circulation, holdings, interlibrary loan, reserves, and e-journals so patrons' needs were identified and met. The system identified shifts so the library could quickly adjust to patrons' changing needs.

Dissemination

Dissemination of assessment results will continue as in-house reports and presentations, journal articles, and conference presentations. New types of dissemination may be used more in the future. YouTube videos may explain how to conduct some specific type of library assessment or to report on results. Blogs, vlogs, podcasts, and other emerging media may also be used, but they are not traditional and fully accepted dissemination methods in the academic community because they lack the rigor of peer-review. Library assessment should also extend to other higher education learning and assessment organizations.

Typical assessment reports describe the reasons for the assessment, how it was conducted, the results, and includes a discussion of what the assessment findings mean to the library, including recommendations. However, assessment reports do not include a plan on how to move forward. This latter part is the purview of library leadership or those responsible for what is being assessed. It is a critical part of assessments to "close the loop." Engberg et al. (2015) indicated that the end result of an assessment should be an actionable strategy and a plan to move forward with the findings from the assessment. This new step should be added to assessment reports so that leadership can outline options and next steps using findings from the report.

Presenting library assessment findings, especially when they connect to improved student learning, at library and non-library centric conferences, brings awareness to how libraries function to support student learning efforts. It raises awareness of how libraries and their assessments may connect to other disciplines and learning efforts. It provides libraries a "place at the table" in regard to all efforts to improve student learning.

Service Value and Decision-Making

Libraries and those who conduct assessments therein are at different places in their journey toward a culture of assessment and accountability. Some libraries have an assessment framework and plans for assessing library services, spaces, resources, and personnel. Some libraries have multiple employees dedicated to conducting or assisting assessments, while in other libraries assessments are only a small part of an employee's duties. Other libraries are struggling to start a single assessment because of a lack of support for assessment efforts or because they have library divisions, departments, or employees that are siloed from one another and do not see the relationships that connect and influence them.

Looking forward requires several key qualities and traits. First, library assessment needs to determine allies within the library. Allies should not be those who want to use assessment results to further their agenda but those who see assessment as a means of understanding what is and is not working. They are willing to admit when they are moving in a wrong direction and take corrective action. Starting with allies helps an assessment program to develop and provides instances where assessment informed decision-making and practice.

Second, efforts should focus on what is doable and actionable. The process of using assessment to inform decisions followed by assessments to confirm decisions goes a long way to indicate the value of assessment in making things not just different but better.

Third, it is essential that collected data and completed assessments are referenced when false or incomplete assertions are made, to show how assessments benefit the library. It is equally important to acknowledge areas that have been over- or under-assessed and to express a willingness to work with under-assessed areas.

Finally, patience is needed on all fronts. Building something takes considerable planning and effort. Slow, steady progress will help to build and strengthen an assessment program as people are convinced of the value of assessment. It is important for those in charge of the assessment program to emulate how assessment should work, namely gathering, examining, and acting on all feedback. Those in charge of assessment should be the most willing to make changes based on feedback.

Summary

The "what's next?" question is used to help those involved with each assessment task look for and improve what and how things are done. Assessments should be like one of those somewhat magical substances that absorbs everything that makes it stronger and better. As library employees begin to accept and use assessments to examine trends and patterns, the power of assessment will become more and more evident. Assessment will not become the end-all and be-all of libraries, but it will inform decisions and planning to help libraries, the people who work therein, and library patrons be the best they can and achieve their dreams

References

Engberg, M. E., Manderino, M., and Dollard, K. (2015). Collecting dust or creating change: A multicampus utility study of student survey. *Journal of Assessment and Institutional Effectiveness, 4*(1), 27–51.

Figueroa, M. A. (2018). Futuring for the future read librarians. *Knowledge Quest: The Future of School Libraries, 46*(4), 15–18.

Hogan, S., and Hutson, J. (2018). Assessing access services: Building a five-year plan for sustainable assessment. *Journal of Access Services, 15*(2–3), 80–88.

Litsey, R., and Mauldin, W. (2018). Knowing what the patron wants: Using predictive analytics to transform library decision making. *The Journal of Academic Librarianship, 44*(1), 140–44.

Washburn, A., and Bibb, S. (2011). Students studying students: An assessment of using undergraduate student researchers in an ethnographic study of library use. *Library and Information Research, 35*(109), 55–66.

Zaugg, H. (2018). Begin again. In M. Britto and K. Kinsley (Eds.), *Academic libraries and the academy: Strategies and approaches to demonstrate your value, impact, and return on investment* (pp. 135–47). ACRL.

Zaugg, H., and Belliston, C. J. (2020). Assessing old and new individual study desks. *Performance Measurement and Metrics, 21*(2), 93–106. https://doi.org/10.1108/PMM-12-2019-0062.

Zaugg, H., and Child, C. (2016). Collaborating with nonlibrary faculty for assessment and improved instruction. *Journal of Library Administration*, 56(7), 823–44.

Zaugg, H., Silva, E., Nelson, G., and Frasier, C. (2020). It looks a bit like this: Prototyping in an academic library. *Journal of Library Administration*, 60(2), 197–213.

Index

Page references for tables and figures are italicized.

About the Editor

Holt Zaugg, PhD, is the assessment librarian at BYU's Harold B. Lee Library. He is responsible for the user experience and process-improvement assessments of library services, spaces, resources, and personnel. He holds bachelor's degrees in psychology and physical education; master's degrees in instructional science and library science; and a doctorate in educational inquiry, measurement, and evaluation. He also oversees the library's internal review process that describes value and recommends improvements to library departments and units. His research focuses on efforts that create a culture of assessment and evaluation within libraries.

About the Contributors

Sheila J. Bosch, PhD, is an assistant professor and graduate coordinator in the Department of Interior Design at the University of Florida. For more than two decades, Sheila has been engaged in research exploring the relationships between environmental design and human well-being, including primarily educational and healthcare environments. Recent publications addressed influences of school layout and design on student achievement and the potential role of design in preventing or mitigating violence against healthcare workers.

Jean L. Bossart, PhD, is the associate engineering librarian at the Marston Science Library at the University of Florida. As a liaison to the College of Engineering, Bossart assists faculty and students with research, data analysis, and investigation and incorporation of creative technologies into the STEM discipline library services. She has an advanced degree in engineering and is a licensed professional engineer. A former research and development engineer, her research interests include engineering education, 3D printing, and environmental sustainability. Recent publications focus on women in engineering and the use of innovative technologies in STEM education.

Adrian P. Del Monte is a Fulbright Scholar and a PhD candidate at the University of Florida, College of Design, Construction and Planning, Interior Design Program. His research interests include design acculturation, vernacular architecture, and spatial and behavioral mapping.

Elizabeth Fields is the research and instruction librarian at Stevenson University and served as the chair of the MD-SOAR shared governance committee from 2018 to 2020. Her research interests include scholarly communication, assessment, and open-access resources.

Barbara Ghilardi coordinates all assessment activities in the DiMenna-Nyselius Library at Fairfield University. She holds a master's degree in library and information science from Simmons University, as well as a bachelor's degree in history from Quinnipiac University. She assists students from all levels of the university with their research needs and serves as a library partner to the Communication Department and the School of Education and Human Development. In her free time, she likes to exercise, watch classic films, and read historical fiction.

Sara Russell Gonzalez, PhD, MLIS, is the physical sciences, mathematics, and visualization librarian and associate chair at the Marston Science Library at the University of Florida. Her research interests include emerging technologies in libraries, modeling and visualization of data, and scientific literacy instruction. She oversees the UF Libraries' 3D service and coauthored the book *3D Printing: A Practical Guide for Librarians* in 2016.

Kirsten Kinsley is an assessment librarian at the Florida State University Libraries and a liaison with the College of Criminology and Criminal Justice, and a coliaison for the Department of Psychology and the College of Social Work. Kirsten completed her master of science in library and information studies in 1999. She received a master of science and specialist in education degrees in counseling and human systems in 1995 from Florida State University. In 1989, she graduated with a bachelor of science in psychology with honors. Ms. Kinsley has been working in libraries on campus in various capacities since 1991.

Joseph Koivisto is a systems librarian at the University of Maryland, College Park, providing centralized application support for the seventeen member campuses of the University System of Maryland and Affiliated Institutions. His research interests include acquisitions workflows, institutional repositories, and digital lifecycle management.

Kelley Martin is assessment and user research coordinator at University Libraries at the University of Missouri–Kansas City (UMKC). She began working at UMKC in 2006 as a sound archivist in the Marr Sound Archives and has served in a variety of positions. As assessment and user research coordinator, she collaborates with library staff to perform user-needs assessments and usability tests. She seeks to improve the library work environment through her knowledge of organizational structure. She has offered presentations on the topic of usability testing, particularly on guerrilla testing. Kelley earned her BA in history from UMKC, an MEd in education technology, and an MLIS from the University of Missouri–Columbia. She is currently chair of the Faculty Welfare and Development Committee and the Camaraderie Committee, and she is a member of the UMKC's Assessment Committee. In her spare time, Kelley tests recipes for *Cook's Illustrated* and the America's Test Kitchen family of publications.

Jason Meneely is an associate professor in the Department of Interior Design at the University of Florida. He joined the department in 2006 from Cornell University, where he worked as a researcher in the Department of Design and Environmental Analysis. Meneely's research examines strategies for maximizing creativity, human potential, and social engagement through the design of the built environment. He also examines values-driven approaches to technology that support human-centered design processes.

In 2019, Meneely received a national Award for Excellence from the Council of Interior Design Accreditation (CIDA) for developing innovative approaches that leveraged virtual-reality headsets to support inclusive design decisions for people with disabilities. He also received the 2012 Innovation in Education Award from CIDA and was recently honored with a UF Term Professorship (2018–2021). He and his collaborators have received a national Research Excellence Award from the Environmental Design Research Association (2018) and Best Presentation awards at the UB Tech (2013), and the Interior Design Educators Council (2004 and 2002) annual conferences. His research has been published in the *Creativity Research Journal* and the *Journal of Interior Design*.

Valrie Minson is the assistant dean of assessment and student engagement and chair of the Marston Science Library at the University of Florida George A. Smathers Libraries. As chair of Marston Science Library, she provides leadership for the only nonmedical science library on campus with 1.4 million visitors per year, supporting forty-two departments across three colleges. Minson's research agenda has included addressing data support services, collection management, collaboration and cyberinfrastructure, and agricultural information services. She is a 2018–2019 Fellow for the Association of Research Libraries (ARL) Leadership Fellows Program. Of additional note is Minson's work as National Implementation Lead and Local Implementation Lead on the $12 million NIH grant funded VIVO: National Networking of Scientists, a multi-institutional partnership to create a Semantic Web application that integrates people, research, and publications into one centralized location.

Susan E. Montgomery is an associate professor and research and instruction librarian at the Olin Library at Rollins College in Winter Park, Florida. She serves as the liaison to faculty and students in several departments and programs including education, international affairs, Latin American and Caribbean studies, and political science. She received her MLIS from Florida State University and holds an MA in Latin American studies from the University of New Mexico and a BA in history and Spanish from Knox College, Galesburg, Illinois. Her research interests include "user experience" and the "library as the third place." She is the editor of the book *Assessing Library Space for Learning* published by Rowman and Littlefield and has published articles in *Journal of Academic Librarianship*, *Colleges & Undergraduate Libraries*, *Public Services Quarterly*, and *Library and Information Research*.

Gregory M. Nelson received his PhD in microbiology and molecular genetics from Loma Linda University and his master's of library and information science from the University of Southern Mississippi. He is the librarian at Brigham Young University over the disciplines of chemical engineering, chemistry, microbiology, molecular biology, neuroscience, and physiology and development biology. His areas of interest include open-access publishing, collection development, library patron experience, and reference assessment. He scholarship focuses on the citation advantages of open access in the field of chemistry, information literacy using flipped classroom approaches, and PDF scan quality of journal backfiles. He enjoys teaching wonderful students in a yearly molecular biology techniques course. He goes to work happy and comes home happy.

Joelle Pitts is the associate dean for administration, planning, and assessment at Carnegie Mellon University Libraries. In that role, she is responsible for library finances, technical services, building operations, human resources, assessment, and reporting. Previously she served as the head of the Content Development and Academic Services Departments of the Kansas State University Libraries. She is a founder and board member of the award-winning New Literacies Alliance, an inter-institutional information literacy consortium dedicated to creating institutional, technological, and vendor-agnostic online lessons. She holds master's degrees in library science and business administration. Integrating her instructional design, collections, and management experience, Joelle's research areas include: distance education and e-learning theory, design, and assessment; inter-institutional collaboration; as well as the intersections of scholarly communication and information literacy. She has published and presented on these topics at the local, national, and international level.

Margaret Portillo, PhD, FIDEC, is professor and associate dean of research and strategic initiatives in the University of Florida's College of Design, Construction and Planning. As associate dean, she provides leadership and service to the college's faculty, centers and research institute, and multidisciplinary doctoral program. Her research program centers on creativity in design contexts and includes the books *Design Thinking for Interiors* and *Color Planning for Interiors: An Integrated Approach to Color in Designed Spaces*. Service during two terms as editor-in-chief of the *Journal of Interior Design* was recognized as significantly increasing the journal's international reach and ranking. In recognition of her body of scholarship, she received a University of Florida Research Foundation Professorship and has garnered national service and scholarship awards from the Interior Design Educators Council and the Council of Interior Design Accreditation.

Laura I. Spears, PhD, is the director of assessment and user experience and is associate university librarian with the University of Florida Libraries. Her job responsibilities include examining a variety of library data that demonstrate library impact on the life of all types of library users. Spears' research examines library value in funding advocacy and values assessment in academic libraries. Recent publications focused on overnight library use perceptions, academic research ethics, and use of Appreciative Inquiry in CoLAB Workshops. Spears works closely with the Academic Assessment Committee to establish and expand the Smathers Libraries' impact. Spears is currently the president of the state's professional organization, the Florida Library Association.

John S. Spencer is currently an associate librarian at Gonzaga University, where he has worked since 2001 as reference services coordinator and currently as an instruction and research librarian. A member of the University

Assessment Committee, he also serves on the Gonzaga Faculty Senate. Previously, he served as distance learning librarian at Central Washington University and as a research support services librarian at Arizona State University (West).

Chuck Thomas is executive director of the USMAI Library Consortium. His background includes twenty-five-plus years in the fields of digital librarianship, digital preservation, and scholarly communication.

Cindy Thompson PhD, is interim dean of libraries at the University of Missouri–Kansas City (UMKC) University Libraries. She began at UMKC in 2006 as the interlibrary loan librarian and took on increasing responsibilities, most recently as associate dean of services and resources, until she attained her current position. As interim dean, Cindy continues many of her former responsibilities, and additionally provides leadership and vision for the development and implementation of the University Libraries' strategic future. A long-time Kansas City resident, Cindy received her PhD from the University of Missouri–Kansas City, her MA from the University of Missouri–Columbia, and her BA from William Jewell College. Her research interests lie with organizational structure and strategic change management, and she is president-elect of the Missouri Library Association and chair of the UMKC Institutional Review Board.

Joshua Tijerino, in his role as the STEM library associate, works with STEM librarians and the rest of the Dirac team at the Florida State University Libraries to support the teaching, learning, and research needs of FSU scholars in STEM disciplines. Tijerino began working at FSU Libraries as a student worker throughout his undergraduate career while simultaneously researching with scholars at the College of Medicine. His future career goal is to become a physician's assistant.

James Waters, in his role as the social sciences, arts, and humanities (SSAH) library operations supervisor, works with SSAH librarians and the rest of the team at the Florida State University Libraries to support the teaching, learning, and research needs of FSU scholars in the social sciences, arts, and humanities disciplines. Waters has worked for the FSU Libraries for over ten years and has provided many services both behind the scenes and on the front lines that have been essential to the FSU community. In one of many critical roles, he managed the library course reserve textbook check out program that provides textbooks for high-failure, high-drop, and high-enrollment courses to undergraduates

Berenika M. Webster, PhD, has been director of assessment and quality assurance at the University of Pittsburgh Library System since 2013. She joined the university from Thomson Reuters, where she managed development of its research analytics products in Australia and the United States. Prior to that, she worked as a faculty member and research administrator in universities in the United Kingdom, New Zealand, and Australia.

Keith G. Webster has been dean of libraries at Carnegie Mellon University since 2013 and was appointed to the additional role of director of emerging and integrative media initiatives in 2015. He was previously vice president at John Wiley & Sons and has been dean of libraries at major research universities in the United Kingdom, New Zealand, and Australia. He served as chair of the National Information Standards Organization in 2019–2020.

Lightning Source UK Ltd.
Milton Keynes UK
UKHW020628241121
394482UK00005B/191

9 781538 149232